Your Team LOVES Mondays ...Right?

A Guide for People Managers ...Just in Case

KRISTIN A. SHERRY

Black Rose Writing | Texas

©2020 by Kristin A. Sherry

All rights reserved. No part of this book may be reproduced, stored in a retrieval system or transmitted in any form or by any means without the prior written permission of the publishers, except by a reviewer who may quote brief passages in a review to be printed in a newspaper, magazine or journal.

The author grants the final approval for this literary material.

First printing

Although the author and publisher have made every effort to ensure that the information in this book was correct at press time, the author and publisher do not assume and hereby disclaim any liability to any party for any loss, damage, or disruption caused by errors or omissions, whether such errors or omissions result from negligence, accident, or any other cause.

Editing: Beth Crosby
Cover Design: Crystal Davies

ISBN: 978-1-68433-463-6
PUBLISHED BY BLACK ROSE WRITING
www.blackrosewriting.com

Printed in the United States of America
Suggested Retail Price (SRP) $17.95

Your Team Loves Mondays (...RIGHT?) is printed in Garamond

*As a planet-friendly publisher, Black Rose Writing does its best to eliminate unnecessary waste to reduce paper usage and energy costs, while never compromising the reading experience. As a result, the final word count vs. page count may not meet common expectations.

To every associate who has had their spirit crushed by a manager,
I wrote this for you.

ACKNOWLEDGEMENTS

"I will give thanks to you, Lord, with all my heart; I will tell of all your wonderful deeds." – Psalm 9:1

Thank you, Xander Sherry. You are the most supportive person I've ever met. This is my fourth book, and you never complain about all the slack to pick up when I take on a new project. I love you like crazy.

Thank you to Mimi Rios. You kept us running like a well-oiled machine at YouMap, LLC, while I was on lockdown for days and days on end, writing.

Thank you to Reagan Rothe, founder of Black Rose Writing, for believing in my project and offering me a contract for this book before a single word was written.

Thank you to Beth Crosby, editor extraordinaire. You always make yourself available to contribute your gifts to yet another one of my projects.

Thank you, everyone who generously agreed to contribute their expertise in interviews with me for this book: Lila Smith, Greg Brenner, Brian Ray, Brenda LaRose, Kimberly Tilley, and Kris Macchiarola.

Thank you to Evans Duren and Nancy Kazmierski for sharing their great manager stories. You bring this book to life through Henry and Petrina's example.

Thank you to the generous people who gave feedback to improve the book: Kimberly Tilley, Julie Leung, and Anna Ziller.

A special thank you to Char Aukland and Lila Smith, my book writing accountability partners. Day after day, I sent you my word count to make sure I'd meet my deadline. You were unrelenting cheerleaders. I'd be remiss if I didn't call out the role you both played helping me rename the book from the original title. Thank you for pointing out, Lila, that it's awkward to gift a book called *Your Team Hates Mondays (Psst...It's You)* to the people managers in your life. We're a soul sister trifecta, and I love you both!

A thank you to Bob Sager, Tony Abbacchi, Lacey Abbacchi, Cory Warfield, Doug Thompson, Zeta Yarwood, Diana Nguyen, Ahmad Iman, Jennifer Spor, Falguni Katira, David Brier, Cathy Bawden, Lori Knudsen, and Tima Elhaj for lending your names in case studies, stories, and examples. Surprise!

A shout out to the folks who contributed stories, quotes and feedback on my LinkedIn posts for me to add to the book: Char Aukland, Esther Adamson, Kay Wakeham, Melissa "Af" Orroyo-Funderburk, Lindy Chapman, Mila Sokolyanskaya, Darryl, Amy M., Jenna, Michael, Steve, Paul, Maya, and Jacob Wierzbicki.

A special call out to Toby Goldstein for being the one person who most anticipated this book's release, asking me regularly how the writing process was going.

So many people motivated me while I was writing the book, asking about its progress, speaking words of encouragement and expressing enthusiasm to read it: Megan Tafolla, Ali Luck, Kimberly Tilley, Raha Sepehrara, Erin Sanchez, Cathy Bawden, Mimi Rios, and many more.

Thank you to my girls for your patience when Mom could manage only 10 minutes of hide-and-seek while writing this book.

Thank you to my mom and dad for everything. I am who I am because of you. I love you.

Thank you to my entire family for their love and support and to my friends for still being my friend even when I spent many weeks on end writing. I am grateful at how understanding everyone is when I drop balls and forget to call when I'm working on a book. You now know I'm a terrible multi-tasker.

Thank you to every person who bought or borrowed this book. There are many ways you could spend your time, and it's an honor you're choosing to spend it with me.

And to anyone reading this that should have been explicitly mentioned in the acknowledgments, thank you for forgiving my oversight. You're in my heart, if not in the functioning area of memory in my brain.

WHO THIS BOOK IS FOR

This book is for you if:

- You want to discover if you will enjoy managing people
- You're not getting the most out of your associates
- You have never learned how to be a good manager
- You want to discover your delegating and directing style
- You want to learn how to adapt your management style
- You're experiencing conflict on your team
- You've made bad hiring decisions
- You have high turnover on your team
- Someone suggested this book and you're taking the hint!

FOREWORD

Many people will say, "Business is just business," and I genuinely believe that is their attempt to justify actions and behaviors that are self-serving and void of genuine connection with their counterparts and clients. I suggest that business provides us a platform to pour into one another's lives and to grow personally through our profession while serving others. Fortunately for me, my first manager taught me what it meant to do just this as I began my sales career.

I hope I never forget that week leading up to my interview with Henry. It was Easter weekend, and I had been home from college to spend time with my family. I was on a roller coaster of emotional highs and lows. I was confident I would exceed expectations and do well in the business, but at the same time, I questioned my odds of landing the job, not having a professional resume to support my ability to perform in such a position.

As I left home for Atlanta, I began to envision how the interview would go. I thought through what questions he would ask, how I would respond, and what questions I would have for him. Hours later, I arrived at the operations facility and walked into the lobby, wearing a seven-dollar pair of pants from Goodwill. Again, the doubts began to swirl. I was sitting in a Fortune 20 company's lobby wearing second-hand pants, an old blazer, and hand-me-down shoes. The odds felt considerably stacked against me.

Waiting for Henry, I kept an eye on the door leading to the back offices. I knew little about sales and almost nothing about the medical industry, but I was ready for this day, for this job, for this opportunity. In my mind, I had to believe the company was more than likely looking for a kid like me with no sales experience and mediocre grades at best.

Before long, Henry and I were discussing everything from the sales territory to my cleaning the floors in the dining hall at night on campus, and running a concession stand for the college's baseball team as my own business. He was more interested in those experiences than my grades, which was great for me.

Towards the end of our conversation, he wanted to know if I had any additional questions for him. Thinking back to my business classes, I asked him what was the company's competitive advantage. Without hesitation, he very matter of fact said, "You are. We are all selling the same products; you're the difference-maker." I later understood he was telling me the customer experience, and the genuine connections we build are what separate us. The products are generally the same but walking alongside my clients in their business would be different from most sales reps. Customers know who genuinely cares about them and who is only there for a sale.

That was the first of many lessons he would teach me.

I lived in Atlanta for the next two months while training before moving to Chattanooga, Tennessee. Six weeks later, Henry called early in the morning and asked if I was sitting down. He explained another territory had opened and wanted to offer me the chance to move there and continue building my business. It was a more developed territory with potentially more opportunity and income. For a young man, newly engaged and trying to establish himself in the industry, I was quick to accept the offer.

Henry was able to work it out so that the company would pay for me to break my brand-new lease in Chattanooga, but I still had to make the move to Johnson City, Tennessee. The company did not cover that part, and the little bit of money I started making was not enough to both move and put down a deposit on my new apartment.

Embarrassed, I explained to Henry I did not have enough money to move and make a deposit. He told me he would write a personal check and for me to handle the logistics of the move. I did not know what to say or how to respond. I had been so confident and sure in my abilities to take care of myself, that it was hard to ask for help and then accept his money.

Henry sent me that check the next day, and his only request was that I pay him back when I was able. No strings attached, no interest, no deadlines, no questions asked. I knew he needed a rep to cover that territory and make sure our company kept its presence and market share. But he believed in me, trusted me to do the right thing, and was willing to support me in my transition. I paid him back within thirty days, and we never spoke of it again.

I worked on Henry's team for two years. I could fill page after page sharing more stories like this. I could tell you how he supported me in my pursuit of becoming the company's national rookie of the year, how he made sure my wife knew what I meant to the company, how to grow a profitable business while creating cost savings for clients, and ultimately how to pour into the lives of the people I served beyond the walls of their businesses.

Henry was my first manager, and I learned many lessons from him that had nothing to do with business. He showed up for me as a mentor, coach, and friend time and time again. I have never forgotten the chance he took on a young man beginning his career and life in the "real world."

When an opportunity arises to pour into someone's life, take it. When you can extend a helping hand while asking for nothing in return, give freely. When someone takes a chance on you, be grateful, and do the same for another.

Henry was great a manager, and I am a better man for knowing him. As you read the pages ahead, I hope his story serves as a testimony to what it means to be the kind of manager who makes a lasting impact on the lives of others.

Evans Duren

October 2019

Your Team L♥VES Mondays ...Right?

A Guide for People Managers .... Just in Case

CONTENTS

INTRODUCTION

"When I finally got a management position, I found out how hard it is to lead and manage people."

Guy Kawasaki, author, speaker, entrepreneur

Managing people is hard. Managing people **well** is harder if you aren't equipped to do so.

In my first management position, I was assigned thirty-one direct reports. Previously, I had been a team lead with delegation and direction responsibilities but no management responsibility.

I learned that I had to think differently than I did as an individual contributor after "stepping in it" a few times. Most of my dropped balls involved neglecting to communicate something to my team or not anticipating how a change impacted them.

When you manage people, you must think further downstream from your team. You might need to create a plan, obtain feedback from your team, and communicate throughout the process.

It's easy to criticize from an armchair. Before I managed people, I had plenty of manager criticisms swirling around in my head. "How could she make that decision?" and "What was he thinking not telling us about that?"

Oh, yes. Finding flaws is easy from that comfy vantage point.

What I didn't realize is how many behind-the-scenes things my manager was responsible for that were completely out of my view. I suppose I thought my managers sat in their offices all day answering team questions and sending annoying emails to the team–the ones doing the real work.

Because of this, I decided to be more intentional in team meetings, providing my team with updates on projects I was working on to increase the scope of their organizational view and offer an understanding of developments beyond their role and responsibilities. I believe it helped my team realize I was juggling a lot of balls and learning the ropes of the team while trying to be open to their feedback.

I'm convinced the majority of people show up to work every day wanting to do their job well. Most managers think they're effective, even if their associates don't agree. Some managers will care and want to do something about it. Others won't. Here are three good reasons why you should care about being an effective manager:

Ineffective managers are a liability to the organization.
Whether your team is under-performing, your turnover is high, or team morale is low, there will come a time when someone higher up concludes you are the common denominator of the issues on your team, which undermines your employment stability. When a sports team continues to lose, the coach is usually held accountable and released more often than the players. Being a competent manager and intentionally seeking ways to grow and improve your skills increases your value as an associate, which benefits your career.

A bad managerial reputation gets around.
People talk. If you're the manager few people want to work with, that opinion is going to make its way around inside–and even outside–your organization. The world has become so small through the internet that with a few clicks, prospective associates can read about your management tactics and interpersonal shortcomings on websites similar to glassdoor.com and vault.com.

Weak managers get in their own way of making a contribution.
If you spend unnecessary time hiring and staffing in response to team members fleeing your team prison break style or dealing with the consequences of low team morale, you aren't bringing value to your team or your organization. You're in a continual pattern of survival: replacing (recruiting, interviewing, hiring, and training) or terminating associates

whose poor performance is likely correlated to demotivation you've contributed to. This cycle doesn't add value to anyone. In fact, it's costing your employer tangible dollars they'd rather not spend on things that have little-to-no return on investment.

I truly care and want to maximize people to be the best they can be. In the spirit of tough love, I will say that if you have poor performers on your team, you, as a manager, are the one responsible. You've either hired the wrong people for the job or failed to properly onboard, train, develop, coach, or respectfully release them.

Only one in ten people are wired to manage others well, according to Gallup's research.[1] Yes, you read that right. In other words, 90 percent of people placed in a manager role are not wired to be an effective manager. Before writing this book, I conducted a global survey with 68 managers. This was a pretty seasoned group, with 62 percent of respondents having more than a decade of management experience.

The graphics below display participants' answers.

I have the following total years of experience managing people:

Less than 1 year	0
1-3 years	4
3-5 years	8
5-10 years	11
More than 10 years	42

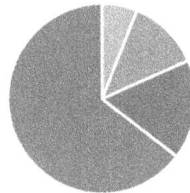

I gleaned interesting insights from the survey, but the one that stood out most was that almost two-thirds of those surveyed never received any formal training when they were promoted to management.

I received formal training on managing people within THREE YEARS of becoming a manager:

No	44
Yes	21

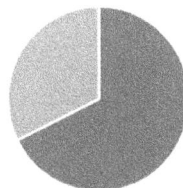

Think about that for a moment. A manager has the single greatest influence on associate motivation, career satisfaction, productivity, and overall well-being. Yet only one in ten people manages well by nature. Is it any wonder manager-associate relationships are such a prevalent problem?

If you're among the nine in ten, and statistically speaking there's a strong chance you are, as I was, my goal is to equip you with the inspiration and information to experience a transformation in your managerial competence.

This book will maintain a positive, constructive, and practical focus to help you uncover your growth opportunities and give you simple tips, tools, processes, and frameworks to become a highly effective manager–or expand the great toolkit you already have–so your team (and you) can love Mondays.

CHAPTER 1

CHARACTERISTICS OF EFFECTIVE MANAGERS

"Effective management is putting first things first. While leadership decides what 'first things' are, it is management that puts them first, day-by-day, moment-by-moment. Management is discipline, carrying it out."

Stephen Covey, author, The 7 Habits of Highly Effective People

When I consider leadership, I think of creating a vision, aligning people to that vision, and championing the execution of that vision.

This book is not focused on leadership. It's focused on management–directing the activities and managing the performance of associates. Often, people will use the terms manager and leader interchangeably. Leaders and managers have different functions, and the world needs competent managers just as much as it needs inspiring leaders. Not all leaders manage people, and not all managers initiate and champion the change leaders do. And that's okay, because we need both. Leaders craft the vision, and managers execute it.

This book will not beseech you to abandon being a "mere" manager and aspire to be a leader. I am meeting you as a current or aspiring manager of people (or an individual contributor looking to do a better job of managing up) and focusing on the core management competencies you need to develop to be successful as a people manager.

Gallup research sheds light on associate-manager relationships, finding that about 50 percent of 7,200 adults surveyed left a job "to get away from their manager."[1] Ouch.

No manager (or person) is perfect. I'm not going to pretend everyone can become an amazing manager everyone adores. Yet everyone has room for improvement. My goal is to equip you to be the most effective manager possible.

For several years, I worked as a consultant, coaching new managers to help them increase their management skills. Most of my time was spent coaching these individuals to manage their own ineffective manager. This is often referred to as *managing up*.

With each person I coached, several unfortunate patterns emerged again and again from ineffective managers:

- Micro-managing behaviors
- Inability or unwillingness to adapt to differences
- Unclear expectations and communication problems
- Lack of support
- Criticism exceeding praise
- Insecurity in his or her role as a manager

Overall, the three top issues I came across when coaching managers were:

1. Lack of awareness of one's own delegating and directing style
2. No interest in adapting to others to achieve better results
3. Communication problems

"Adapt to others" is not a recommendation to alter your personality or become someone you're not. *Harvard Business Review* reports that Edwin E. Ghiselli's study on management talent revealed, "Managers who adopt artificial styles or follow practices that are not consistent with their own personalities are likely not only to be distrusted, but also to be ineffective."[2]

Your management approach should be consistent with your personality while learning to modify your behaviors. The idea of adaptive behavior might seem an overwhelming or difficult concept. Adapting to others is about choosing the behaviors that are likely to bring the desired result in a specific situation. How we must adapt will be unique, depending on our unique design–how we're wired–as well as the person we're adapting *to*.

One's management style is shaped by a variety of factors, and this book focuses on the following six:

1. **Personality**
2. **Strengths**
3. **Values**
4. **Preferred skills**
5. **Experience**
6. **Emotional intelligence**

We will review these six factors in depth in the chapter, "Discover Your Management Style." In the meantime, I've created a simple formula called "The 3 C*s*" to help you focus your attention on the three most important characteristics that increase your effectiveness when managing people.

The 3 Cs

If you ask one-hundred people the most important characteristic of a good manager, you'll probably get seventy-five different answers. (The same holds true if you ask those same people the worst quality of an ineffective manager.) I asked that question on LinkedIn and hundreds of people responded. I discovered the answers fell into one of three categories, which is how I came up with The 3 C*s:*

Character, Competence, and Caring.

Character refers to the moral and ethical qualities of a person. This includes traits such as honesty and truthfulness, patience, respect, and fairness. Focusing on consistent demonstration of respected character traits creates trust with your team.

Competence is the ability or capacity to perform one's management responsibilities capably. This could include proper delegation without micro-managing, addressing conflict on the team, and knowing how to deliver feedback effectively.

Competence doesn't mean knowing it all or never making mistakes. Admitting you're wrong or that you don't know an answer, then promptly following up with accurate information, is vital to being perceived as a competent person.

Caring relates to having concern for others. Your associates must believe you care about what's important to *them*. This includes having compassion for their needs and preferences such as their need for support, independence, or collaboration, as well as compassion for things outside the workplace, such as an associate going through a family situation such as divorce or caring for a chronically ill child.

Developing The 3 *Cs* is not enough to usher in your success as a manager, but it's a solid foundation to build the trust you need to operate from. Miscommunication can create conflict that could call your character, competence, or caring into question, despite your intentions.

For expert communication insights, I interviewed Lila Smith, creator of the Say Things Better™ method of intentional communication based on her work as a professional actress in theater.

Lila had a lot of astute things to say and shared original and fresh insights that I hope you'll find thought-provoking, motivating, and useful. She started by sharing the top two priorities managers should have when considering how they communicate.

"Communication comes into play in management in two main ways: preventing and creating. You want to **prevent** drama and negativity, and you want to **create** safe space and accountability.

"When you're looking to prevent a meltdown, a lot of people's instincts are to altogether avoid a confrontation. Conflict will feel different to various kinds of managers; some people will see things as confrontational when they aren't confrontational to others. Disagreements will be viewed through the lens and filter of that manager.

"If someone is afraid of confrontation, sometimes they add in an apology or over-apologize for what they're about to say. One of the greatest challenges for managers is communicating through issues related to expectations and accountability. Managing expectations, being clear about them up front *first*, before you hold somebody accountable, is step one. You must make sure associates know what's expected of them.

"Next, you have to empower associates with actions and information, fair pay and treatment, and a safe workplace environment. You must also set up agreements ahead of time when you're welcoming them to your team and your environment. This way they know how, why, and when to come to you, and what it will feel like when they do.

"That's why I create safe spaces with Verb Your Values™, using the verbs that we can agree to "do" when we're in a space together. You can do things like set a time for open office hours or allow someone to make an appointment. You can tell them, 'During this time we can speak about this thing specifically or anything that's going on for you,' to keep expectations the same on both ends. You have this time to have discussions and, during this time, here's what it's going to feel like. As a manager you must model openness and appreciate their feedback.

"Being clear about expectations before you even have a meeting means that people know they will have a chance to express themselves, and it doesn't have to be in the heat of the moment. If you are providing feedback in the moment, say, to a team member who is not being constructive in a meeting, you should ask yourself whether it's something you must mention in front of other people, or if it's something that can occur in private. Unless it's a physical safety concern, you can put a stop to negative communication as it's going on.

"If other people are at risk of being hurt in the room because you're allowing someone else to go on a diatribe, you can stop that immediately but still provide acknowledgment. Any time someone's hurt or communicating from a negative place, you still want to acknowledge their feelings matter. You can say, 'Joe, I feel your stress here. I understand where you're coming from, but this conversation isn't going to be productive, and we have other things to work on. Let's set up a time for a conversation. Why don't we start with just you and me talking about it, and then we can bring other people in if we need to.' You're acknowledging what's happening, but you're also putting a stop to it before it gets all over everybody else.

"When you're in trusted working spaces, you'll want to do things to encourage innovation, ideation, and idea sharing while coming from a place of diversity and inclusion to actively seek ideas that are different from your own. You have to prepare in advance for those ideas to feel uncomfortable, because they weren't yours. We're very comfortable with our own ideas. We're not necessarily comfortable with other people's ideas.

"Yet, when other people's ideas and opinions are allowed at the table, both your mind and theirs might open. People feel open to hearing your ideas only if they feel their own ideas are valued as well. That's the same for introverts and extroverts, for everyone. Everybody wants to feel that they and their voice matter. You also can't make somebody have something to say when they don't. You can't pull something out that's not there.

"When you are in meetings, you can set the expectations ahead of time: 'We're actively seeking diverse voices. We're looking for diverse ideas. We're not going to shoot anything down, so let's hear everything and be appreciative.'

"When we choose our values, maybe we choose "to thank" whether we're speaking or we're silent. Our values can be expressed in alignment with one another if they are our true intentions. If I go into a room agreeing to appreciate everybody who is in that room, and I have that up on the board in front of me, it's a lot easier to remember a two-word reminder: to thank, to absorb, to reflect, and/or to expand.

"Place the 'yes' verbs on one side of a white board and the 'no' verbs on the other. Examples of 'no' verbs would be to diminish, to detract, to patronize, to criticize, and to dismiss. On one side is how we agree to communicate from a place of intention, and the other is how we agree not to. It's just a visual reminder to hold us accountable in high stakes moments. It's helpful for both feedback sessions and innovation sessions."

Have you set intentions, expectations and agreements how the team will and will not communicate? This kind of intention is powerful. When I was managing a large operations team, I set an intention that our team does not participate in gossip. I set the expectation that we address issues directly, and I equipped the team to do so in two ways.

First, I led a personality workshop to help the team understand our different needs and motivations. I pointed out that we can interpret someone's behavior as purposefully trying to make our life difficult when they are merely seeking to have their needs met at work, as we all do.

Second, I led a training session on how to have difficult conversations, complete with simple scripts on how to broach sticky topics. I gave them language to say things such as, "I'd like to see if we can create a better understanding about _____. I want to hear your thoughts and share mine as well."

I asked Lila to share her thoughts on the importance of effective managers receiving feedback from others. We see a lot of advice out there on how to give feedback but not as much on how to be effective at receiving feedback.

Here is what Lila shared in our interview.

"I once reported directly to the owner of the company, a C-level executive. My experience with his feedback was that it was always delivered in a way that felt like he had been personally offended by something I had done and that he didn't agree with, whether it was a style of work, or a work product, or the way that I handled something. The feedback would always be an attack. So two things happened:

1. I learned that I could not have a close relationship with him and that I could not trust him to have effective conversations with me.

2. I learned how to mine and interpret his feedback into something actionable, so that if I were going to stay, and I did for multiple years, I would have a way to strategically use his feedback and never give him the chance to say that I didn't try to take his advice to heart.

"It was his company so, ultimately, what he says goes. I can run my company my way now, but when I was working for him, I needed to be able to manage up in this way.

"Managing up for me, being in this abusive conversation, which was always offensive, still gave me a tool for interpreting feedback into something actionable, getting his confirmation and sign off that, yes, I did understand what he said. That built more trust between the two of us even though he had severe issues trusting anybody to do good work, which was why he was micromanaging and having personal offense carry through to his communication. It was always very erratic, but it did build more trust when I would listen for the content of what he had to say.

"It's very hard to hear the message of what someone is saying when the feeling of what they're saying is so offensive. But it doesn't mean that it's impossible. When you are managing either up, down, or laterally, you always have the option when you get feedback to mine for information.

"In theater, I learned to conduct dramaturgical research where we would look at the script to mine for information without judging the characters, because they're fictional. We don't have any kind of personal relationships with them, and there are no personal stakes in our real lives if they are, or aren't, a certain way. So we removed judgment and doing this gave me a tool to interpret feedback for myself. I remove the personal. I can, even in my head, black out with a mental sharpie marker any words that are offensive, until I only have the main message in terms of what can be actioned out.

"Here are some negative words. Here is a negative tone. What would it look like if, instead of hearing his tone and seeing his angry face, this were written in a script? What would it look like if I saw only the words? Which words would I have to remove to find the useable information?'

"Then, I would cross those words out until I found exactly what it was that I needed to understand. You learn in a script that lots of other characters will say things about your character when she's not around. That doesn't make those things true about her. It makes them true to the other characters' experience of her. It was my responsibility as an actress, just as it is for a manager or associate, partner or friend, to be considering the full picture of who I know myself to be. This helps explain why people who are different than me view me the way they do.

"This helps you to depersonalize and de-escalate a situation; looking at it from function instead of feeling, and strategically move forward with the information, if there is any forward motion to be made.

"This is how you can take responsibility for your side of the communication, even when someone else is abusive or seemingly impossible."

Let's reflect a moment on what Lila shared. Is there someone you work with whom you can practice depersonalizing, de-escalating, and moving forward with actionable information by mining for the core message and removing the words and tone that aren't constructive? Think of a recent conversation you've had that didn't go well and try to apply the process Lila described.

In the chapter, "Develop: Maximize Potential," I'll cover providing feedback to others.

If you're interested in more excellent communication content, follow Lila Smith on LinkedIn at www.linkedin.com/in/lilasmith.

In the next chapter, "Assess Your People Management Fit," I'll help you decide if management is the right path for you.

CHAPTER 2
ASSESS YOUR PEOPLE MANAGEMENT FIT

"The higher we are placed, the more humbly we should walk."

Marcus Tullius Cicero, Roman philosopher

The first step to decide if managing people is right for you is heightening your self-awareness of your strengths, values, preferred skills, and personality, which shape your delegating and directing style and offer insight into whether managing people is something you'll enjoy.

It's important to note you can be good at something and still not enjoy doing it. Plenty of good managers advocate for their associates, invest in them and champion them, but the experience comes with a great energy cost. There is a misconception that if we're good at something, we should do it. If something drains your enthusiasm for your work, why do it?

In February 2019, I received this message through social media from Rachel, a former direct report on my team from 2010–2013:

I wanted to share with you what you have done for me. It started when you were my manager. I immediately was drawn to you and knew I was blessed to have time with you as my leader. I grew monumentally because of your wisdom and guidance...which allowed me to "skip" a level and obtain that program manager job I desired and earned because of you. Now, 18 months after that program manager promotion, I am starting my next chapter as a SENIOR program manager! Your words, guidance, advice, and books resonate with me in everything I do. I eagerly hung on your every word during our meetings and documented everything you advised. I truly know that you were the one person who guided me to use my talents and build up my shortcomings to make me the strong person I am today. So I thank you. Thank you from the bottom of my heart. If you ever need an example of what can be accomplished with your guidance...I'm your girl!

This message meant so much to me because it appeals to one of my most important values: making a difference in people's lives. Yet, make no mistake, managing people is a burnout skill for me. I do enjoy mentoring and coaching people *who report to someone else*. People are wonderful, but the activities of people management drain me.

People become managers for many reasons. Before I started writing this book, I conducted a survey asking people who have managed others (now, or in the past) *why* they became a manager.

Two reasons tied for number one.

"I was given the promotion."

"It was the logical next step in my career."

I became a people manager because (select all that apply):

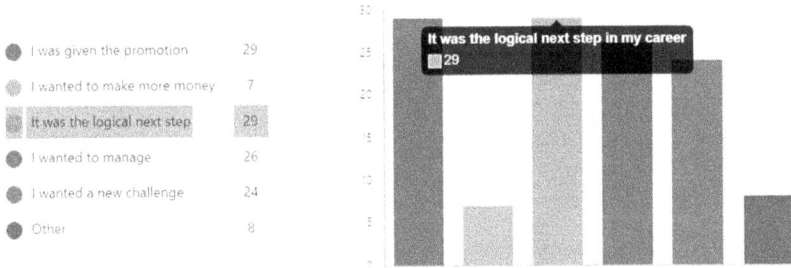

I was given the promotion	29
I wanted to make more money	7
It was the logical next step	29
I wanted to manage	26
I wanted a new challenge	24
Other	8

It was the logical next step in my career
29

These aren't awful reasons, but they aren't exactly the best. They seem so unintentional. Interestingly, "I wanted to make more money," had the fewest votes in the survey. So that was encouraging!

Did those surveyed want to be a manager? Did they believe management aligned with their strengths? When I asked these same respondents if they felt that, overall, they were a good manager, 85.7 percent agreed or strongly agreed they were good managers.

What's interesting is that Gallup states that companies miss the mark on hiring high managerial talent in **82 percent of their hiring decisions**.[1]

How can so many companies miss the mark? As I mentioned in chapter one, according to Gallup's research, only one in ten people possess high talent to manage others.[2] Put another way, 90 percent of people *do not* possess high talent to manage others. Yet almost 86 percent of the people who responded to the survey believe they're good managers. And maybe many of them are. But given Gallup's research, it's more likely that managers are not aware of their blind spots, or they've never been given straightforward feedback about their management strengths and challenges.

The Kanizsa Triangle

Take a close look at the following image. How many circles and triangles are there?

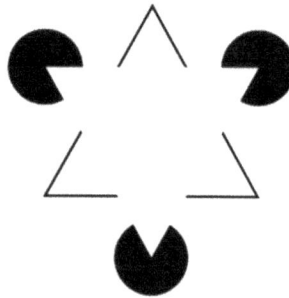

Gestalt psychologists use something called a Kanizsa Triangle to describe what they call the law of closure, which suggests that objects grouped together are interpreted as a whole. In other words, we perceive objects as whole even when they are incomplete. This occurs because we disregard gaps and complete outlines in our mind to form familiar patterns. For example, in the Kanizsa Triangle, we are quick to perceive two triangles and three black circles, even though there are precisely zero circles or triangles drawn.

The Kanizsa Triangle illusion challenges our reductionist tendencies, since what we see in the image is not the sum of its parts. We see more. Specifically, we perceive things that are not there. This tendency beautifully illustrates our blind spots as people and, yes, as managers. We see things that are not there about ourselves and others.

One way we do this is we assign patterns (often negative ones) to behavior in others that might not be a pattern at all. For example, we interpret one or two instances of a person showing up late for a team meeting over the course of an entire year as a pattern of tardiness, even if the person showed up early 96 percent of the time.

Alternatively, we see positive patterns of behavior in ourselves that might not be patterns at all. We see our way as the best way and might not notice problems with our management style. These errant beliefs might include thinking we've made our expectations clear when we haven't, failing to recognize we're managing people too closely, or being too hands-off with our team.

Awareness of your inherent strengths and challenges as a person and as a manager, offers an opportunity for intentional personal and professional development to maximize your effectiveness.

In the next chapter, I'll go into more depth to help you increase your self-awareness and assess your strengths and challenges to reveal where you will excel or might struggle as a manager and share insights to help you find if management requires things of you that will leave you burned out and unfulfilled.

Take a free quiz to evaluate if management is right for you: www.glassdoor.com/blog/manager-quiz

CHAPTER 3
DISCOVER YOUR MANAGEMENT STYLE

"Our prime purpose in this life is to help others. And if you can't help them, at least don't hurt them."

Dalai Lama, Tibetan spiritual leader

In "Characteristics of Effective Managers", I introduced six factors that can affect how we manage people. In this chapter, I'll address each of the six management style influences in more depth:

1. Personality
2. Strengths
3. Values
4. Preferred skills
5. Experience
6. Emotional intelligence

Personality & Management

There are no good or bad personality styles; all are equally valuable, and people of all personality types can become effective managers. Likewise, every personality type can contribute to problematic management behaviors. I'll discuss the strengths and challenges our personalities can present when managing people, along with example scenarios and tips to increase effectiveness.

Your Delegating & Directing Style

Our personalities can explain our natural tendencies, including how we are inclined to delegate and direct the performance of others, two core responsibilities of a manager. These natural tendencies shape our *priorities*.

According to the Wiley Everything DiSC® Management Profile, a personality assessment that reveals personality-based management style, managers have **eight core priorities**:

1. Challenge
2. Drive
3. Taking Action
4. Encouragement
5. Collaboration
6. Support
7. Reliability
8. Objectivity

These eight priorities determine what comes natural to us and how we approach managing people. I'll review the four types of the four-factor model of personality (D, I, S, and C) and their corresponding priorities. As I discuss each type, think about managers you've had. Which style sounds most similar to them? Were they easy or challenging for you to get along with? Reflect on your own personality as well. Which manager type's priorities do you relate to?

You might find you relate to more than one type. About 85 percent of people will have a primary and secondary type, while 15 percent of the population is predominantly found in just one of the four types. For example, I am both the D and I types, which means I shift between the priorities listed under both the D and I managers.

I'll share example scenarios combining several styles in reporting relationships to illustrate how various personalities have challenges working together. After sharing the example scenarios, I'll offer three tips for increasing effectiveness with direct reports of each of the four styles.

D Manager Priorities

- Challenge
- Drive
- Taking Action

Managers with the D style place an emphasis on holding people accountable, driving results, and getting people moving to pursue bottom-line results. Overall, they respond best to people who can quickly help them achieve success.

D manager tendencies:

- Might overlook people's feelings or compromise quality due to a drive for results
- Prioritizes action and wants to keep moving at a fast pace
- Challenges the status quo, pressures others to meet high standards

I Manager Priorities

- Taking Action
- Encouragement
- Collaboration

Managers with the I style are energetic and encourage others to do their best. Overall, they want to lead a fast-paced but friendly team and respond best to people who enjoy creating an optimistic team spirit.

I manager tendencies:

- Gives recognition and celebrates group victories
- Prefers to work with others and prioritizes teamwork
- Focuses on action and moves quickly while striving for progress

S Manager Priorities

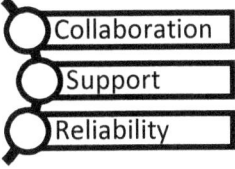

- Collaboration
- Support
- Reliability

Managers with the S style are accommodating and dependable. Overall, they want to lead a team in a calm setting where tension is rare. They will often respond best to people who are friendly team players.

S manager tendencies:
- Emphasizes support of others and empathy for people's needs
- Prioritizes collaboration, wants people to work together in harmony
- Often avoids change to maintain a dependable setting

C Manager Priorities

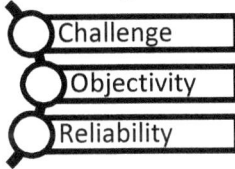

- Challenge
- Objectivity
- Reliability

Managers with the C style place strong emphasis on logic and maintaining a stable environment. Overall, they want to lead by setting high standards, and they will often respond best to people who share their concern for high quality outcomes.

C manager tendencies:
- Will spend a lot of time on objective analysis to ensure accuracy
- Moves cautiously to deliver a reliable outcome
- Will show open skepticism for ideas that are not backed by facts

Again, which manager's priorities do you most identify with? This influences how you interact with your direct reports and how they respond to your management style.

Your Management Style and Your Direct Reports

The D Style Manager

If you are a **D** style manager with a **D** style direct report:

Chances are you'll work well together. Your direct report will have similar priorities of **challenge, taking action,** and **drive**. Therefore, a task-oriented and rapid approach to work is not likely to cause strain.

If you are a **D** style manager with an **I** style direct report:

You have the shared priority of **taking action,** so you both will have a sense of urgency to get projects moving. However, your associate tends to be accepting and warm and prioritizes **collaboration** and **enthusiasm**.

A management approach that is too direct and task-focused can cause your associate to become detached and disinterested.

If you are a **D** style manager with an **S** style direct report:

You will have no shared priorities with your associate, who prioritizes **collaboration, support,** and **reliability**. With no shared priorities, these two styles have the potential for the most conflict.

A management style that is too fast-paced and independent can cause your associate to feel overwhelmed and unsupported.

If you are a **D** style manager with an **C** style direct report:

You have the shared priority of **challenge,** so you both will have a tendency to challenge yourself and others. However, your associate also prioritizes **objectivity** and **reliability**.

A management style that moves too fast toward results without time for due diligence can cause your associate to become skeptical and resistant.

The I Style Manager

If you are an **I** style manager with a **D** style direct report:

You have the shared priority of **taking action**, so you both will have a sense of urgency to get projects moving. However, your associate tends to focus on **drive** and **challenge**.

A management style that is too enthusiastic and collaborative can cause your associate to become frustrated by what they perceive as too much socializing and not enough results.

If you are an **I** style manager with an **I** style direct report:

Chances are you'll work well together. Your direct report will have similar priorities of **taking action, enthusiasm** and **collaboration**. Therefore, an energetic, fun and fast-paced approach to work is not likely to cause strain.

If you are an **I** style manager with an **S** style direct report:

You have the shared priority of **collaboration**, so you will enjoy teamwork as a way to accomplish results. Your direct report also prioritizes **reliability** and **support**.

A management style that is too fast-paced and spontaneous could make your direct report anxious about too much change and less secure in her ability to perform her role.

If you are an **I** style manager with a **C** style direct report:

You will have no shared priorities with your associate, who prioritizes **challenge, objectivity,** and **reliability**. With no shared priorities, these two styles have the potential for the most conflict.

A management style that is too spontaneous, fast-paced and relational will be in opposition of their methodical, consistent, and fact-based approach to work.

The S Style Manager

If you are an **S** style manager with a **D** style direct report:

You will have no shared priorities with your associate, who prioritizes **challenge, drive,** and **taking action**. With no shared priorities, these two styles have the potential for the most miscommunication.

A management style that is cooperative and seeks to create a stable environment can cause your associate to interpret your approach as indecisive, conflict avoidant, and standing in the way of progress.

If you are an **S** style manager with an **I** style direct report:

You have the shared priority of **collaboration**, so you will enjoy teamwork as a way to accomplish results. Your direct report also prioritizes **taking action** and **enthusiasm**.

A management style that tends to be slower-paced and change averse could frustrate the creativity, enthusiasm, and action-orientation of your associate.

If you are an **S** style manager with an **S** style direct report:

Chances are you'll work well together. Your direct report will have similar priorities of **collaboration**, **support,** and **reliability**. Therefore, your consistent, cooperative, and supportive approach to work is not likely to cause strain.

If you are an **S** style manager with a **C** style direct report:

You have the shared priority of **reliability**, so you both have a sense of accountability and do what you commit to do and enjoy a stable work environment. However, your associate also tends to be focused on **challenge** and **objectivity**.

A management approach that is focused on cooperation over facts and logic can frustrate the associate's need for independence and logic.

The C Style Manager

If you are a **C** style manager with a **D** style direct report:

You have the shared priority of **challenge**, so you both will be comfortable challenging each other. However, your associate also tends to be focused on **drive** and **getting results**.

A management approach that is more slow-paced and data-driven can cause your associate to become frustrated with the slow pace and methodical processes that get in the way of getting fast results.

If you are a **C** style manager with an **I** style direct report:

You will have no shared priorities with your associate, who prioritizes **taking action, enthusiasm,** and **collaboration**. With no shared priorities, these two styles have the potential for the most conflict.

A management style that is too calculated, logical and task-oriented will cause your associate to become demotivated if he is unable to take a spontaneous, energetic and relational approach to his work.

If you are a **C** style manager with an **S** style direct report:

You have the shared priority of **reliability**, so you both have a sense of accountability to do what you commit to do. However, your associate also tends to be focused on **support** and **collaboration**.

A management approach that is too focused on logic and data can cause your associate to think you are cold and unsupportive.

If you are a **C** style manager with a **C** style direct report:

Chances are you'll work well together. Your direct report will have similar priorities of **challenge, objectivity,** and **reliability**. Therefore, your conscientious approach to work with a methodical pace is not likely to cause strain.

Personality Case Studies

Scenario #1: D + I Personality in Action

Diana was strongly oriented in the "I" style, reporting to Ahmad, who was a strongly oriented "D" style. During meetings, Diana became talkative and expressed enthusiasm and excitement about ideas and how the team might collaborate to get started. Ahmad's body language, pursed lips, shifting in his seat, and terse demeanor resulted in Diana assuming Ahmad didn't like her or take her seriously.

After the meeting, Ahmad gave Diana feedback that she was too enthusiastic in meetings and suggested she tone it down. In future meetings, Diana felt uncomfortable and became self-conscious of her reactions, worrying she was too expressive and talkative for Ahmad's liking. Meetings became stressful with her sensing the need to monitor her reactions too closely. She became discouraged and questioned if others considered her unprofessional. Diana became self-conscious and demotivated and rarely spoke in meetings going forward.

What went wrong?

Because Ahmad prioritizes challenge, drive, and taking action, he wants to get to the point in meetings to get results. Diana's talkative nature seems like time wasting to someone with a bottom-line goal and Ahmad's tendencies. Since Ahmad doesn't prioritize expressiveness, he cut right to the chase when delivering feedback to Diana.

On the other hand, Diana values a high energy, expressive environment, working collaboratively toward a goal. And she wants to be liked. Ahmad's feedback resulted in Diana thinking she was not permitted to express herself and that Ahmad didn't like her. This probably was not the case, and Diana personalized Ahmad's preferences as having something to do with her, when it very likely wasn't personal at all.

Scenario #2: D + S Personality in Action

Zeta was a strongly oriented "S" style reporting to Dan, who was strongly oriented to the "D" style.

Zeta was also a people manager, and in a recent meeting with her manager, Dan, she brought up a decision she had to make then shared her thoughts and asked Dan his opinion.

Dan responded, "Zeta, you're supposed to be a leader. I can't make your decisions for you." Zeta was stunned and insulted but didn't openly address her concerns with Dan. Instead, she left the meeting in silence.

What went wrong?

Dan's tendency is to make decisions independently, and he values taking quick action.

As an S, Zeta prioritizes collaboration and support. Zeta is not incapable of making decisions, she prefers a collaborative decision-making approach, which is why she asked Dan for input. Zeta felt unsupported in response to Dan's comment. Remember, support is one of the three priorities of the S style.

Because Zeta also prioritizes support, she tends to avoid conflict instead of openly sharing how Dan's response affected her. As a result, Zeta builds silent resentment toward Dan as she perceives her priorities of collaboration, support, and stability are disregarded and undervalued by Dan.

Scenario #3: I + S Personality in Action

Tony was a strongly oriented "I" manager, and his assistant, Cory, was a strongly oriented "S" style.

On Monday mornings, Tony burst into Cory's office sharing about his weekend, laughing, and talking a mile a minute and quickly shifted into the tasks he needed Cory to complete that day. Then he abruptly announced he was running late for a meeting, gave Cory a thumbs up, and said, "Catch you later!"

Cory immediately became stressed, and his face showed visible blotchy patches that resembled a heat rash.

What went wrong?

Cory prioritizes support, collaboration, and reliability. Tony's ready-fire-aim directions for Cory's tasks did not allow him to ask questions for clarity. Because the S style wants to offer support behind the scenes and reliably deliver tasks they are given, the ambiguity of Tony's off-the-cuff direction caused Cory stress. Tony's in-your-face enthusiasm and loud manner of speaking, especially first thing in the morning, overwhelmed Cory.

The S style does not enjoy conflict, so they might not speak up and instead silently resent management styles that make them anxious.

Scenario #4: C + I Personality in Action

Falguni was a strongly oriented "I" associate reporting to Jennifer, a strongly oriented "C" style manager.

Falguni and Jennifer got along at first, but it wasn't long before conflict surfaced. When Jennifer delegated tasks to Falguni, Jennifer managed her very closely to instruct how to accomplish a task, shooting down all Falguni's ideas. She gave Falguni feedback that she was completing tasks incorrectly, regardless of delivering the result expected. Jennifer had specific preferences for how tasks should be approached based on her own personality.

Because Falguni was creative and spontaneous, the methods Jennifer dictated didn't mesh with her work style preferences. Falguni became increasingly frustrated and expressed her thoughts to her manager. Jennifer became defensive, and Falguni felt her feedback was being ignored.

Eventually, Jennifer began writing up Falguni for not performing tasks as she had directed, and Falguni was let go.

What went wrong?

Jennifer prioritizes challenge, objectivity, and reliability. Falguni prioritizes taking action, collaboration, and encouragement. Falguni's less structured and more spontaneous approach to her work caused Jennifer to lose confidence in Falguni's ability to get the job done right, even though Falguni was capable of delivering the expected result. Because Falguni responded with her feelings about the situation, instead of a more fact-based approach, Jennifer disregarded her opinions.

Scenario #5: S + C Personality in Action

Jacob was strongly oriented in the "C" style, reporting to Tima, who was a strongly oriented "S" style manager. Jacob prioritized challenge, objectivity, and reliability. He tended to challenge assumptions and make decisions using logic. Jacob was most concerned with doing things accurately to create an efficient and stable environment.

Tima also valued stability, but she prioritized being supportive and collaborative. Recently, Tima's team was tasked with creating a new program offering for customers. Tima set up a series of meetings to listen to input from the team and collaborate on solutions that best support the client.

Jacob became frustrated with the number of meetings he was asked to attend and gave feedback to Tima that the meetings were unfocused, unproductive, and full of irrelevant chatter from the sales team. He did not hide his displeasure when stating the meetings were a waste of time.

Tima was uncomfortable and hurt by Jacob's direct and matter-of-fact style. To avoid drama, she apologized to Jacob and said she would try to improve the meetings.

What went wrong?

Because Jacob is concerned with doing things correctly and maintaining a stable environment, a meeting without a clear agenda, schedule or defined objectives introduced a lot discomfort for a C style associate. Talkative extroverts in attendance combined with a lack of meeting structure set the stage for what Jacob considered an unproductive meeting.

Because Tima valued stability, support, and collaboration, Jacob's approach to feedback felt cold, detached, and critical. Tima could have improved the situation by asking Jacob to attend meetings only where his feedback or analysis was required. Having a clear agenda with set objectives could prevent Jacob from becoming frustrated.

Increasing Your Management Effectiveness

Small adjustments to how we interact with our direct reports (or everyone, for that matter) can make a big difference in the effectiveness of our working relationships. Effective managers can adjust to the needs of their associates. Adjusting your style isn't about changing your personality; it's about adjusting your behavior to best fit a situation and bring about a better result.

Following are tips to improve your working relationships, by style.

Tips to work better with a D direct report:
The D style is happiest when independently working at a fast pace, focused on achieving results.

1. Give them freedom to decide tactics for accomplishing a goal
2. Increase their autonomy and decision-making as they gain experience
3. Encourage and allow them to take on greater challenges

Tips to work better with an I direct report:
The I style is happiest when working in a high momentum, collaborative, and enthusiastic environment.

1. Acknowledge their contributions publicly
2. Support their creativity and experimentation while ensuring they meet deadlines
3. Give them plenty of encouragement

Tips to work better with the S style:
The S style is happiest when working in collaborative, supportive, and stable environments.

1. Demonstrate sincere warmth and friendliness
2. Give them clear instructions and offer support
3. Give them enough time to complete tasks without feeling rushed

Tips to work better with a C direct report:
The C style is happiest when working in objective, accurate, and stable environments.

1. Avoid opinions unsupported by facts
2. Allow autonomy but set clear, reasonable deadlines
3. Avoid forcing collaboration unless necessary

A solid starting place is to first focus on what you have in common with your direct report(s). Next, consider adjustments you can make based on the priorities you don't share with them.

Now that you've reviewed tips to work better with direct reports, this is a good time to pause and reflect.

Has your management style clashed with a direct report due to personality differences? Use the space given to name the style, or priority of the style, with which you've experienced conflict.

Which of the tips given could you use to modify your approach to increase effectiveness?

Capture your thoughts

_____

_____

_____

_____

_____

_____

_____

_____

_____

_____

_____

_____

_____

_____

_____

_____

_____

Strengths & Management

The world of work is changing, and a big driver behind that is the burgeoning gig economy. If this term is new to you, a gig economy is "…a free market system in which temporary positions are common, and organizations contract with independent workers for short-term engagements."[1]

Automation will continue to remove the more routine aspects of a role and, in the case of managers, people management skills are becoming more important than ever. These short-term engagements give rise to an increase in matrixed organizations with managers serving as a functional manager, directing and delegating to the project team, while there is often a project manager who is managing the project comprised of cross-functional team members from across the organization.

Project-based organizations reduce the relevance and effectiveness of traditional organizational hierarchies and give way to the democratization of work. We will begin to see a more power-balanced workforce with managers shifting from the role of boss to that of a performance coach.

Effective managers will assess individual strengths of team members and, rather than focusing on weaknesses, help them succeed by providing opportunities to use their strengths and regular performance feedback.

The best way for a manager to start with a strengths-based approach is understanding his own talents.

We lack objectivity and awareness of our own strengths because we're born with these talents and often don't realize the things we do naturally are, indeed, talents. If you've never taken a strengths assessment, I recommend Gallup's "Clifton StrengthsFinder." I've debriefed thousands of people, individually and in groups, on their strengths and across the board, people find this information incredibly helpful, powerful, and relevant.

The first insight to know concerning your strengths is the kind of strengths you possess. Natural talents are categorized into four themes:

Relating – How you build one-on-one connections, with others
Influencing – How you move others to action
Executing – What pushes an individual toward a result
Thinking – How a person analyzes the world

The first two categories (Relating and Influencing) are people-facing or outward-focused strengths. The last two categories (Executing and Thinking) are inward-facing strengths, internal to you.

I have four Thinking and one Influencing strength. My Influencing strength is called Maximizer. I enjoy helping people move into roles where their potential can be lived out. Therefore, I was good at developing people, and it's why I became a coach. But because four of my talents are inward-focused, spending a lot of outward-focused time with people drains me, even though I'm good at it and enjoy it.

If you take the "Clifton StrengthsFinder" assessment, the second important insight will be the specific strengths you possess. You'll learn a lot regarding how you approach managing people based on your strengths, including why it energizes or drains you.

Gallup has conducted extensive research on high performers in diverse roles from top military personnel, teachers, bank tellers, and truck drivers. One commonality Gallup has discovered among top performers across all roles is successful people have similar talents, and managers are no exception.

Gallup describes manager talent using these five talent dimensions:

Motivator – bring out the best in people, keep others enthusiastic and involved
Assertiveness – express yourself effectively and stand up for your point of view, while respecting the rights and beliefs of others
Accountability – take responsibility for your own actions
Relationships – effectively build social connections

Decision Making – ability to decide outcomes of options and determine which choice is the best for a situation

According to Gallup, these five dimensions of manager talent are the greatest predictors of performance across different industries and types of manager roles, such as general manager, field manager, and team manager.

"An individual who exhibits the five dimensions to a high degree has what Gallup calls 'high' manager talent. An individual who has many of the talents necessary to be a successful manager but needs support has 'functioning' talent. An individual who lacks talent across the five dimensions has 'limited' talent and is much less likely to be a successful manager regardless of the support he or she receives."[2]

In the "Emotional Intelligence" section of this chapter, Kris Macchiarola, an emotional intelligence practitioner, will touch on a few of these traits in more detail.

Values & Management

Our values are our determination of what is important to us. Values guide our decisions, actions, and ability to influence other people. Having clear values leads to increased confidence and decreased stress, because values help you lead a life aligned with what matters to you.

Knowing your values and aligning your actions with them gives you tremendous personal power to create boundaries, make better decisions, and authentically interact with others in accordance with your values.

I'll share my top five values here to illustrate how they shape my management style:

Love/Connection – It's important I am connected to my own manager and my direct reports. I remember when I was an individual contributor, I once reported to a manager whom I respected and liked. However, he didn't have one-on-one meetings with his direct reports. I remember telling him if we didn't have a regular touch base, I wouldn't have a connection with him, and could become demotivated. I hadn't done my values at that time, but I was unconsciously attempting to live them out.

Making a Difference – Everywhere I've ever worked, I sought out opportunities to help people reach their potential. I helped a lot of people resolve conflict, get promotions, or increase their confidence by shining a light on their greatness. Making a difference and leaving a lasting impact on people lights my fire. My favorite way to make a difference has always been through mentoring.

Autonomy – I enjoy being self-governed and want to accomplish my tasks my own way. I prefer to work independently rather than collaborate. This is the biggest reason I left corporate life. I wanted to work on my own goals and not be forced to collaborate on projects I wasn't passionate about. I reciprocate autonomy to those who report to me and never micro-manage people, because I can't stand to be micro-managed myself.

Fun – Laughing and having a good time is important to me. I enjoy injecting fun into the mundane, and I approach life with light-heartedness. When I worked in the corporate world and moved to a new team or office, I'd get emails from people who used to sit near me telling me they missed hearing the laughter coming from my office.

On Cinco de Mayo, I showed up to the office in a huge sparkly sombrero and sarape and handed out maracas to my team with our program name carved in them. If there's no fun, I don't want to be there. Not everyone shares this value. I once had an associate who told me she just wanted to do her work and go home. She wasn't at work to make friends. The nature of her job didn't require collaboration, as she was helping patients over the phone. I was happy to oblige her and didn't take it personally. She had different values.

Freedom – I can't stand the thought of being imprisoned. To me, freedom extends to being able to think and speak my mind. I don't enjoy environments where people aren't free to share their thoughts or where healthy conflict is actively discouraged. I have always told my direct reports they are welcome to say anything to me.

How do your values shape your management style?

Preferred Skills & Management

Our preferred skills tell us how we want to spend our day.

The table that follows displays 55 common skills. Notice that Leadership and Supervise are separate categories. As shown below, leaders initiate change, lead others, mentor, and motivate. You can have an interest in leading people without supervising them. (This is me!) Examples of this are a project team lead or a specialized consulting role such as a Six Sigma Black Belt or management consultant.

Conversely, you can be interested in managing people without crafting the vision. In other words, some managers aren't interested in initiating, but instead implementing a leader's vision, as I discussed at the beginning of chapter one, "Characteristics of Effective Managers."

Administration	Leadership	Sales
• Budget	• Initiate Change	• Competitiveness
• Categorize	• Lead Others	• Negotiate
• Organize	• Mentor	• Present/Perform
• Paperwork	• Motivate	• Risk-Taking
		• Sell
Conceptual/Creative	**Manage Process/Projects**	**Supervise**
• Abstract Thinking	• Customer Service	
• Ambiguity, Deal with	• Execute	• Decision Making
• Create Images	• Expedite	• Delegate
• Design	• Handle Change	• Hiring/Staffing
• Envision	• Manage Logistics	• Manage Others
• Ideate	• Manage Time	
• Improvise	• Monitor	**Technical & Mechanical**
• Innovate	• Multi-Task	
• Strategize	• Plan	• Computer Skills
		• Edit
Interpersonal	**Research & Analysis**	• Estimate
		• Mechanical
• Advise	• Analyze	• Numeric Accuracy
• Collaborate	• Assess	• Test
• Instruct/Train	• Interview for Information	• Write
• Liaise	• Observe	
• Manage Emotions	• Research	
• Mediate	• Study	
• Use Intuition		

With this skill exercise, you can assess how you prefer to spend your day. You should aim to spend at least 80 percent of your day using preferred skills.

Below are the 55 skills in list format. Read each skill and its definition.

If you **enjoy and are good at a skill** place a check (✔) next to it. If you **don't enjoy** the skill (even if good at it) place an "X" next to it. If unsure, skip the skill.

Abstract Thinking – Form and develop ideas and concepts

Advise – Provide counsel, guidance, direction, information, or enlightenment to others

Ambiguity, Deal with – Can act when details are unclear, comfortable leaving issues open, at ease with the unknown

Analyze – Examine methodically and in detail, typically for purposes of explanation and interpretation

Assess – Evaluate, assess, or judge to determine quality or capability

Budget – Estimate costs, revenue, and resources over a specified period

Categorize – Arrange people or things into classifications according to shared qualities or characteristics

Change, Deal with – Embrace or deal well with change to work priorities or focus

Collaborate – Willing to follow or lead, shows trust and support of coworkers; builds partnerships

Competitiveness – Enjoy challenging goals, being measured against those goals; strong desire to win

Computer Skills – Use computers and related technology such as Microsoft Office efficiently, with a range of skills

Create Images – Illustrate through drawing, sketches, photography, or other visual means

Customer Service – Assist, advise, and solve customer problems and support customers appropriately

Decision Making – Frequently decide outcomes of options and determine which choice is the best for a situation

Delegate – Assign tasks to others; explain why a task is important and the expected results

Design – Plan the look and function or workings of a program, product, or object before it is created or made

Edit – Read or revise written or printed materials

Envision – Picture or envision what's possible

Estimate – Roughly calculate or determine the value, number, quantity, or extent of

Execute – Implement and follow through on policies, plans, or programs

Expedite – Restructure actions or solve problems to accomplish tasks quicker

Hiring/Staffing – Good judgment about people; make selection decisions that result in good performers

Ideate – Generate or think up ideas

Improvise – Perform or think on one's feet, that is, without planning or preparing

Initiate Change – Introduce or influence new ways of doing things

Innovate – Welcome, encourage, and seek continual improvement on a small or large scale

Instruct/Train – Show or explain to someone how to do something

Interview for Information – Ask questions using insight to obtain information

Lead Others – Enjoy taking responsibility and directing others; take charge of introducing necessary change

Liaise – Communicate or cooperate between people or organizations to facilitate close working relationships

Manage Logistics – Manage events; handle detailed coordination of people, facilities, or supplies

Manage Emotions – Ability to realize, readily accept, and deal with the feelings of others

Manage Others – Directly manage others and provide performance feedback

Manage Time – Able to use one's time wisely and productively to meet deadlines

Mechanical – Repair, fix, or operate machinery

Mediate – Intervene between people in a dispute to reach agreement

Mentor – Guide, coach, or counsel less experienced associates or students

Monitor – Track people, activity, or information to confirm fairness or correctness

Motivate – Bring out the best in people; keep others enthusiastic and involved

Multi-task – Deal with more than one task or project at the same time

Negotiate – Attempt to reach an agreement or compromise with others

Numeric accuracy – Solve numerical problems, work with numbers, or look for patterns in numbers

Observe – Notice, see, perceive, discern, and identify something observed as significant

Organize – Keep work area neat, follow an orderly approach, and keep things organized

Paperwork – Comfort with repetition and attention to detail and maintaining accurate and timely records

Plan – Specify steps for a project before beginning and prepare for potential problems before they occur

Present/Perform – Speak or perform in front of an audience

Research – Engage in data discovery such as conducting online research

Risk-Taking – Willing to leave one's comfort zone; focus on reward over potential for failure

Sell – Ability to persuade and promote; optimistic and does not take no for an answer

Strategize – Able to identify long-term goals; work backward to identify the most effective option of the alternatives

Study – Read written information in a thorough or careful way

Test – Examine critically to determine accuracy, precision, or quality

Use Intuition – Able to understand something immediately using insight without need for conscious reasoning

Write – Make an effort to put thoughts in writing; is concise, descriptive, and keeps readers in mind

After completing your checklist of preferred skills:

- Highlight or underline all skills you selected as preferred in the skills table.
- Note the categories where your preferred skills are most concentrated.
- Pay attention to skills listed under Supervise and additional skills in the Interpersonal category commonly required for management: advise, instruct/train, manage emotions, mediate, use intuition, monitor.

What do your preferred skills tell you concerning your interest in managing people?

Experiences & Management

Our experiences, good and bad, influence the kind of manager we become. Some of us have had excellent managers who shared wonderful principles to emulate and incorporate into our own management style. Others have had a slew of challenging managers who taught them what *not* to do when managing people. Still others pass the torch of negative examples learned and, perhaps unknowingly, embed negative management practices into their behavior.

I've been fortunate to have had mostly good or neutral managers. No one is perfect, and I believe we should give our managers grace because, again, it's difficult to manage people well, and everyone is going to make mistakes.

When I think back on my own managers, I've learned core lessons to guide what I will and will not do, which is largely centered around my values. This is my management manifesto:

I will…
- Help people see and reach their potential
- Tell people the truth and deliver difficult messages compassionately
- Give people the benefit of the doubt and not make assumptions

I will not…
- Treat people disrespectfully
- Neglect to demonstrate compassion
- Micro-manage others

Have you ever taken time to reflect on the lessons you've learned from the managers you've reported to? Your management manifesto is your written declaration of your intentions and motives as a manager. In the space below, I encourage you to list managers you've reported to and reflect on the following questions to create your management manifesto.

What did they do well? What did they do poorly? As a result, and based on your values, what behaviors could you add, or remove from, your management style? Once this is complete, create your own management manifesto in the space provided.

Capture your insights:

_____

_____

_____

_____

_____

_____

_____

_____

_____

_____

_____

_____

_____

_____

_____

_____

_____

My Management Manifesto

I will...

●

●

●

I will not...

●

●

●

If you're willing to be vulnerable, you could share your management manifesto with your team for accountability. If not, consider sharing it with someone you trust, such as a mentor.

Emotional Intelligence & Management

When you become a manager, your success no longer depends on yourself. Your success depends on your team. This means you must expand your emotional intelligence beyond yourself to recognize, empathize, and influence the emotions of your team.

Justin Bariso, author of *EQ Applied,* defines emotional intelligence, also known as EQ, as making your emotions work for you instead of against you. I highly recommend this book if you're interested in real-life stories about EQ with practical application.

Google has a website, https://rework.withgoogle.com, which is a collection of practices, research, and ideas from Google and others to help you put people first.[3] Among the many useful resources on this site, one I especially appreciate is a guide called *Care Professionally and Personally for Your Team.*[4]

This guide includes a section titled "Understand Emotional Intelligence and Compassion." This section offers six tips for managers to cultivate compassion:

• Ask how you can help and don't assume you know what's wanted.
• Look for commonalities with your team members.
• Encourage cooperation instead of competition in your team.
• Cultivate a genuine curiosity about the individuals on your team.
• Lead by example; treating others with compassion is contagious.
• Be mindful of boundaries; avoid being an emotional sponge.

Why should you care to cultivate compassion? Research by Christine Boedker from the Australian School of Business found that EQ and, specifically, compassion in managers, had the greatest impact on organizational profitability and productivity.[5]

I recently had the pleasure of interviewing Kris Macchiarola, author of the incredible book *#NoApprovalNeeded* and an EQ consultant who helps companies cultivate emotionally intelligent leaders. I asked Kris to share common issues she sees with managers in the area of emotional intelligence. Here's what she had to say on the topic of EQ and managers: As a manager, you must be able to be assertive. If you can't be assertive, then you're not going to be able to communicate in a direct way to get people to understand what you want or the resources you need. A lot of people end up in a management role that lack the skill of assertiveness, and that's a problem. They avoid direct communication, they allow interpersonal conflict to become a problem, or they resort to email and instant messaging to communicate, because they're uncomfortable having direct conversations with people.

If you recall in the section, "Strengths & Management," Gallup cited assertiveness as one of the five talent dimensions critical for managers.

Kris continues:

Something I commonly see that trips people up is equating assertiveness with abrasiveness, and they're totally different things. Assertiveness just means being direct with respect. As team members, we prefer our supervisors to be direct with respect with us. We want to know where we stand. We want to know what they're looking for. Whether it's interpersonal conflict, telling people what your expectations are, or doing a performance review, how can you be effective as a manager if you can't be assertive?

You'll always be beating around the bush on the passive side, or you're on the aggressive side, and you're being abrasive. There are two ends of the spectrum, and you really want to be operating in the middle. I think the easiest way to do that is to remember direct with respect means considering someone else's feelings. You're considering their communication style, and you're flexing your communication style to deliver the content of that message in the best way possible, so it's received the way you want it to be received.

Another issue I see is empathy. When I think about assertiveness, I think about a coin. On one side you have assertiveness, and on the other you have empathy. You should always be using both in tandem to make sure you're balanced. You don't want to be a victim of your own behavior.

Empathy is your best tool for turning an adversarial relationship or conversation into a collaborative one. When we don't like someone, or we have a problem with them, it's easy to turn off that empathy switch.

What I tell people is if you find yourself frustrated with someone, you don't want to talk to them, and you'd rather shut communication down, use that as a red flag alert for yourself that you've turned your empathy switch off. Engaging in this practice will increase self-awareness and the need to connect by assuming good intentions and asking good questions. It's difficult to assume good intentions and seek to understand without empathy.

When you're delivering your message, you should be looking for the cues of the people receiving it:

What is their body language saying?
What is the tone of their voice?
What is their facial expression?
What are the words they've selected to say to you?
Is your message being received the way you intend?
Are you listening more than you speak?

I also see people avoid assertiveness a couple of different ways. They either equate it with abrasiveness and bite their tongue because they don't want to be viewed as abrasive, or there's a relationship trigger and interpersonal conflict. It becomes important to hold yourself accountable to think about work relationships and conflict the same way you would about any other problem or task.

You want to break it down into goals for a conversation. "By the end of the day today, I'm going to reach out to Kristin, and I'm going to talk to her about these one or two things, and by the end of the conversation I want to gain agreement on [whatever it is]."

If we allow these things to fester, or avoid communicating, it just blows up. Avoidance never works. It's never a good strategy because resentment builds and miscommunication increases. These things are so avoidable if we can just hold ourselves accountable to do what makes us uncomfortable.

You also must be very careful with writing. Our brains are trying to decipher intent and tone, and we have a limited amount of information, so we misinterpret what's going on very easily.

In my conversation with Kris, she shared five key areas measured in the EQ-i 2.0 model of emotional intelligence, a well-known emotional intelligence assessment: self-perception, stress management, decision-making, self-expression and interpersonal. Each of these five categories has three sub-scales.

Kris explained that many people are not aware how they score across emotional intelligence traits until they see their results.
"Sometimes people are initially resistant to undergo an evaluation for their emotional intelligence but, by the end, everyone who initially resisted is glad they did it and found it helpful. They often say they didn't understand how emotions come into play in their work and thought emotions should be separate from business.

"With intention, awareness, and practice, all these areas can be improved. Every day we have an opportunity to practice. When we're not getting the outcomes we want, that's when it becomes even more important to start getting curious.

What was my role in creating this outcome?

Are there any patterns here?

Are there triggers for emotions and actions that resulted?

What happened before? Label the emotion.

What was my response/reaction?

What was the consequence or outcome?

"We can begin to recognize patterns and make different choices so that next time, instead of allowing our emotions to oversee how we react, we can oversee our emotions."

One of the things I found most fascinating about my emotional intelligence conversation with Kris was the research on salary. Emotional intelligence helps you use emotions to your competitive advantage, which becomes a performance differentiator.

Kris shares the following regarding financial indicators and EQ:

We have 30 years of research, and we know people that score high on emotional intelligence are high performers. Ninety percent of high performers score high on emotional intelligence. There's also research from Travis Bradberry that for every point increase in emotional intelligence there's a $1,300 difference in pay. The people who score high in emotional intelligence make about $30,000 more per year.

It makes sense. These are the people who relate well to others, that make sound decisions, that are not allowing stress to consume them. They have self-awareness so they're closing the deals, they're getting the promotions, and they're earning the merit increases. They're able to articulate what they need to be successful. IQ can get you in the game, but EQ is what differentiates your performance.

During our interview, Kris discussed one of her first clients who was an ER physician. He was off the charts brilliant, but he alienated everyone around him. She told me when they first met, he believed everything that was going wrong at work was everyone else's problem. He accepted no personal accountability.

The client didn't make eye contact with Kris when she tried to coach him. During the engagement, Kris had him doing homework finding two people each day to connect with on his break. She instructed him to ask people about their kids, hobbies, or movies, whatever it took to find something to connect with them.

Interestingly, he began to enjoy the exercise because people started to realize he wasn't such a jerk, and his coworkers began responding differently to him. By the time he was done working with Kris he had made a few friends! Not only that, his patient satisfaction scores improved drastically, and the attending physicians who reported to him gave better reports, because he wasn't so argumentative with them. Instead, he was engaging the skill of empathy and listening to the opinions of others.

As Kris said, every day is a chance to practice building your EQ skills. If you're interested in more content on EQ, follow Kris Macchiarola on LinkedIn at www.linkedin.com/in/kris-macchiarola.

CHAPTER 4

ASSOCIATE DEMOTIVATION: 7 CAUSES

"Everyone has an invisible sign hanging from their neck saying, 'Make me feel important.' Never forget this message when working with people."

Mary Kay Ash, entrepreneur

An important blind spot managers must remember is how he or she might demotivate an associate who was once motivated. I have coached associates who accepted a new role with high enthusiasm and energy only to watch them, before my eyes, quickly spiral down to a place of indifference because of the dynamic between them and their direct manager.

Interestingly, in many cases, the manager appeared to believe they made a bad hire based on the conversations taking place with the associate. I have been involved in coaching relationships where the associate had been a top performer and when the new manager was put in place, everything changed.

These managers did not connect the dots of their management style that influenced their associate to lose motivation. A manager cannot motivate an associate. Workers need to be self-determined and driven. Yet the environmental conditions a manager creates can absolutely strip a person of her motivation.

Research from the University of California found that motivated associates were 31 percent more productive, had 37 percent higher sales, and were three times more creative than demotivated associates.

They were 87 percent less likely to quit, according to a Corporate Leadership Council study on more than 50,000 people.[1]

UK-based recruiting firm, Michael Page, cites the following seven causes of associate demotivation,[2] which are consistent with my leadership and management consulting experience.

Lack of flexibility

I once worked for a company where the culture was committed to remote work as a cost-reduction and associate retention strategy. It was very common for front-line associates up through executives to work from home. I joined a team where the manager was not enamored with the remote work policy. My peers and I often joined meetings from our office while most of the other attendees joined the meeting from their home offices.

Despite our collective, repeated efforts to influence a remote-friendly team culture that aligned with the organizational remote-work culture, the best we were able to achieve was two work-from-home days each month. One of my coworkers had a daily four-hour commute, which resulted in hospitalization from blood clots forming in her legs due to the amount of time she spent sitting.

Being flexible in our preferences is an easy way for our associates to believe they're appreciated and, in many cases, being flexible costs us nothing.

Have your associates been asking for increased flexibility in any areas where you could adapt and give more flexibility?

Short-term objectives with no career vision

The work a manager needs accomplished through a role is a priority. Yet motivation will erode in the long-term if an associate doesn't believe the accomplishments they desire to make, the level or position they wish to obtain, or the difference they want to make is taken into consideration.

Career vision takes into account the big picture of an associate's career, while short-term objectives are "in the weeds" without bringing that big-picture vision into view. Start with the organization's mission. Help the associate see how their short-term objectives contribute to the organization's mission, while in parallel, helping your associate develop a long-term vision for their career based on the needs of the organization and what the associate does best. The intersection of the associate's knowledge, skills, and abilities combined with the future needs or areas of growth in the organization is an ideal union.

Sometimes the associate's vision outgrows your organization, and sometimes your organization's needs outgrow the associate. With regular touchpoints regarding the associate's career vision, no one is caught off guard when the organization's and associate's goals no longer align.

It should be expected the next step for some associates will be to leave the organization. That should not be a threat to you as a manager. When a team member leaves, opportunity is created for someone else. A complete step-by-step plan to help your associates build a career vision will be laid out in the chapter, "Develop: Maximize Potential."

Feeling undervalued

The book, *Appreciation: Celebrating People, Inspiring Greatness*, cites research that found recognition and appreciation is the number one thing associates say their boss can do to inspire them to produce great work.[3]

Some people need more recognition than others, while people high in humility are often uncomfortable with public recognition. You can be certain that insincere recognition that lacks meaning to the individual will not be valued.

One practice I started early in my management career was asking my team members how they wanted to be recognized and rewarded. For example:

- Monetary rewards and bonuses
- Public recognition
- Words of affirmation, praise, or thanks
- Increased authority or decision-making
- Special stretch projects and increased responsibility
- Paid time off
- Awards

Is it possible you have associates on your team who might not think they are valued? What is one action you can take to be more proactive and intentional to make each of your team members believe they're valued?

For further reading, check out *The 5 Languages of Appreciation in the Workplace: Empowering Organizations by Encouraging People* by Gary Chapman.

No development opportunities

It's engrained in most people to want to grow. This isn't just my opinion. It's based on data I've gathered over the past two years. One of the four pillars of career satisfaction is our values, or what's most important to us. My company's YouMap® profile helps people uncover their strengths, preferred skills, interests, and define their top 10 prioritized values. Our data reveals "growth" is the third most common value, behind making a difference and meaningful work, which tied at number one, and love/connection at number two.

I'll discuss practical ways to help your associates create a career vision in the "Develop: Maximize Potential" and "Retain: Value Your Treasure" chapters.

Poor leadership

Do you recall what I said earlier regarding the work of a leader? Leaders cast a vision, build alignment around the vision, and then champion the execution of that vision. When associates are working in an organization that doesn't have a clear vision, it's hard for them to understand where the organization is going and how the work they do fits into that picture.

Robert Greenleaf, founder of the modern servant leadership movement, said long ago, "The great leader has a ready answer to the profound question: What are you trying to do?" A leader's visions of the future will excite the imagination of others, and they will be inspired because of what you can help them see. A vision brings others hope and optimism. Someone needs to have a sense of where the department or organization is headed. If leadership is caught up in the day-to-day, associates will lose faith.

Yet good leadership goes beyond having a vision. Creating a flexible, inclusive environment supported by clear communication where everyone knows they can contribute is vital.

Conflict

Anywhere you have people, you'll have conflict. Managers can sometimes create conflict, either directly with associates, or with a management style that pits associates against one another. Some managers might even ignore conflict or workplace bullying, which creates a hostile workplace environment.

Dubai-based workplace culture consultant Dawn Metcalfe's book, *The HardTalk™ Handbook,* is an outstanding resource to learn how to handle difficult conversations. I'll touch on difficult conversations in the feedback section of the "Develop: Maximize Potential" chapter.

Unrealistic workload

You might be tempted to think unrealistic workload means having too much work to do. The opposite will demotivate associates: not having enough to do, or not enough challenging and interesting work to do.

It can be difficult to figure out how much your team members have on their plates when you're not in their shoes. When delegating tasks or projects, it's important to ask your direct reports to proactively decide when they've reached capacity and help them prioritize.

Now, let's be sure you hire the right people for the right roles right from the start!

Chapter 5

Hire: Right People. Right Roles.

"The main way to reduce stress in the workplace is by picking the right people."

Jesse Schell, CEO, Schell Games

During a conversation I had with consultant and business strategist, Dave Pennington, about the importance of hiring the right people into the right roles, he remarked, "People hire from their gut. And they hire people they like. When you don't have clarity about the job, you will adjust the role to fit the person."

This is so true, and I've been guilty of doing this myself when it wasn't in the best interest of the team or, even worse, the role no longer mapped to the competencies that were most needed.

Darryl, a leader in the pharmaceutical industry, shared the following:
At a previous job, I had someone who struggled in one aspect of practice but excelled in another. The task they excelled in was generally an easier, less stressful one. By maximizing their talents and putting them in the role that they excelled in, they became very good at it and helped the department overall with this task. But it alienated everyone else.

Others became upset that they had to do extra work because the person wasn't able to contribute to the more challenging things in the department. It brought morale down. So, I strongly believe in maximizing people's talents. It goes along with helping others grow, it brings good publicity to the group, and it even creates succession plans. But there has to be a balance between helping the one person versus helping the whole group or department.

There is a hospital/healthcare leadership coach, Quint Studer, who points out that it is easy to get sucked into putting your time into your low performers, but you really should be rewarding your high performers and getting your middle performers up a level and getting your lowest performers out of the organization.

Sometimes, adjusting a role to fit the person works out, and other times it's a disaster because the person can't do what the role requires, or the rest of the team resents the concessions made for one team member, affecting morale, as Darryl experienced.

What tends to happen in hiring is that a recruitment campaign takes place where selection is based on a good resume and a good interview.

Research by Leadership IQ showed only 19 percent of new hires are an unequivocal success, with half failing in the first 18 months.[1] The reason is not skill-based. It's largely poor interpersonal skills such as coachability and temperament. Studies by Michigan State University's School of Business confirm these high failure rates. They found if an employer ensured the right people were selected for the right jobs in the first place, recruitment success rates increased to 90 percent.

The point is hiring outcomes improve when we explore not only the experience of candidates, but their aptitude, values, competencies, and personality.

In addition to reviewing hiring research, I conducted interviews with people who possess deep experience in human resources and recruiting. One person I interviewed, with a staggering amount of hiring experience, is Brian Ray. Brian has interviewed more than 25,000 people in his career.

Brian's long and distinguished career includes experience as the former Vice President of Support Services at Chick-fil-A corporate offices and leading his own executive search firm placing talent from managers up through C-suite and board of director positions.

Brian's role at Chick-fil-A involved overseeing human resources, independent operators to run stores, and the recruiting and selection process of home office staff. Brian shared the following thoughts on hiring: When I first got to Chick-fil-A, we were getting 10,000 serious inquiries annually, which was a lot at the time. I brought in a consultant to do an analysis, and what we found out was, first and foremost, the thing that made the biggest difference [in a successful hire] was a personal referral.

If somebody came in and used the name of someone in the company, the odds of them being successful were 42 times more likely that they'd be hired and do well. Therefore, we made a major shift in where we started prospecting. Instead of being reactive, waiting for someone to come through a buddy, we started equipping our managers and our operators to make it easy for them to refer.

The second thing we did was spend an extraordinary amount of time figuring out who was going to be a great fit for our company and the role to be filled. That was number one, because if you don't get that right, you can't train and develop them to be the right person.

We took what was a one-page application and made it an eight-page questionnaire. And we noticed a huge drop in inquiries-to-applications. Many people weren't willing to fill it out–and it was an easy application. And then we used phone screens to further qualify and then met them in person.

Character and competence were the two things we were watching out for. Within a year we increased the quality of our candidates.

Brian's experience at Chick-fil-A illustrates a number of great points, and it never occurred to me that making the application lengthier deterred candidates from completing the process because they weren't committed or serious. Much emphasis is placed on making the application process easier with endless complaints on social media about having to complete online forms with information already found in the resume. Perhaps not all instances of rigor in the process are bad if hiring managers seek a certain kind of person for the culture.

It makes sense that referrals lead to better quality candidates. If you have accountable associates, it follows they refer people of similar character. The only caution with referral programs is to be cautious of referrals leading to homogeneity in your workforce. Thought diversity is important for any organization to be competitive and innovative.

Next, I asked Greg Brenner to share his thoughts on hiring. Brenner has 15 years of human resources experience and is an assistant vice president of talent and organizational development at the University of Miami.

Here is what he had to say on hiring:

At an organizational level, hiring hinges on your organizational philosophy for how you bring talent in. In your own world of your department, controlling what you can control, how do you handle that new person coming in?

For instance, what's your process on how you're going to find the right people and, even before that, do you have the right roles? Is the role going to help you do the work that you've been asked to do? What is it you need from the right people?

Some work that we're doing is around a model called "The Suitability Model," created by Dr. Elliot Jacques. The suitability model looks at:

1. Knowledge, skills and attributes. Does the person have them for the job?
2. Can they process information at the level the role expects and requires?
3. Do they have the right temperament for the role?
4. Do they accept the responsibilities of the role?

If there's a kink in any one of those, it doesn't mean it's a no. It just means you might have some issues with fit with that person for the role.

Where you run into trouble with associates is typically around temperament, or they can't process at the level you need them to for that role. Or sometimes, they think the work is below them, so they don't accept responsibility.

You can train the skills, but those other things may not be a fit for that role.

A common theme has surfaced! Both Brian and Greg emphasize the importance of getting the right person into a role because it becomes difficult, and sometimes impossible, to influence a fit where there isn't one. This underscores the importance of a solid behavioral interview process, because three of the four pieces of the suitability model can't be gathered from a resume.

Brenda LaRose agrees.

She is the third person I interviewed on hiring. Brenda is a Chartered Professional in Human Resources (CPHR), a Certified Management Consultant (CMC), and partner at Leaders International, a global executive search firm with a niche specialty placing indigenous executives in C-suite and board of director positions. She has more than 30 years of experience in search and recruiting.

Brenda's backstory is inspiring, and she gave her permission to share it with you:

I was always in recruiting and staffing, and I went to work in the community for an initiative to help with employment for indigenous people. I knew I wanted to go into executive search, and I ended up getting a couple of offers and was hired by a search firm with 11 people. I approached the owners and said, and this was 25 years ago, "I think there's an opportunity for us to do search in the indigenous community."

They responded, "We don't think there is."

When you're doing search or consulting, you have to be billable 80 percent of the time, and 20 percent is meetings, training, development: anything that's not billable. They told me I could develop the (what was then called) aboriginal executive search component, "But you can't do it on our time, not even in the 20 percent. You have to do it on your own time."

So I said, "Okay, I'll do that."

After two years, about a third of the revenue coming into that firm was from business that I got through indigenous executive search. And the people in the firm were not knowledgeable about the indigenous community, so we did some cross-culture training.

What happens in our [indigenous] community is, when they find out what you do, they're probably not going to make an appointment. They're going to drop into the office with their resume. I'd have one person a week coming in without an appointment.

One day, on a Friday, the two women owners called me into the office and said, "We're an HR consulting firm, and you cannot have these native people coming into our office and sitting in the waiting room."

I went home, and I was a single parent at the time so money was tight, but I thought "I absolutely cannot go back to work there." I went in on Monday. I resigned and gave two weeks' notice. I thought, "I'll give starting my own firm a try doing this work, and if it doesn't work by September, I'll go and find another job."

But it worked. I hung up my shingle, I told people, and it boomed. And I think it was about a month later I had to hire a couple of people. I had no inkling or idea to start my own company. I wasn't interested in that, and I never would have done it if that hadn't happened.

As a career consultant, I've heard so many stories of rejection being redirection, but Brenda's story is, hands down, one of my favorites.

In our interview, we discussed hiring the right fit, diversity, equity, inclusion, and bias in hiring. One of the first questions I asked Brenda was, "What, in your vast experience, are the drivers for making a good (or poor) hire?"

Brenda answered, "Your map is really the competencies for the role and the skills and experiences needed to be successful, but you need to have a good understanding of the culture of the organization, and you have to understand the objectives and goals over the next three years. Nothing goes beyond three years now, since everything's changing so quickly. You need to understand the personality of the manager the person will be reporting to. What kind of a leader are they? How do they prefer to work?"

Next, I asked Brenda if clients ever go against her recommendations and make a poor hiring decision.

"If I don't think a client should hire someone, I will tell them. And I've been in that situation. Either the person hasn't performed at the interview stage, or something has come to light.

"About seven years ago, a client wanted to hire a chief operations officer, and he wanted a specific person that we'll call Sam. Sam was highly qualified and was working in another organization, but I had heard of some issues with Sam. He had a good track record, but at that time Sam was not in a good place and had some addiction issues. So, I said to the CEO, 'We'll do a search, and I'll talk to Sam.'

"Sam applied, and the CEO just wanted Sam. He didn't care about any of the other people we were bringing in, even though they were all highly qualified, and there were two or three that would have been much better than Sam. The hiring manager was set in his ways. He wanted Sam.

"It was good that the board was involved, and when we got to the interviews, Sam did well, and I said to the CEO, 'I need to turn him inside and out. I've heard some information he's going through some hard times, and it's not going to be a good fit for you.'

"So I went to all the references, and I found out from four of his six references that he's got a problem with depression where he won't come into the office for long periods of time, and he's got some addiction issues with drinking. This came out in black and white in his references, and the CEO still wanted to hire Sam.

"I told him we needed to have a call with the selection committee, and I shared the references and that my recommendation was not to hire Sam for those reasons. The hiring leader convinced the selection committee to hire him anyway, and I said on the phone, 'If you hire Sam, we cannot offer you a guarantee and replace him because the references are clear.' And, of course, Sam didn't last seven months because of his issues. They had to terminate him for the same reasons we were able to show in the references.

"People form an impression, and this is where confirmation bias comes in—when they're seeking and finding evidence that confirms their initial belief. He made a decision based on availability bias, the most top of mind information he had about Sam from when he first met him. He ignored the evidence that would change that belief.

"The flipside is a negativity bias. The CEO had a positive bias toward Sam, but sometimes our negative biases about different demographics are in play, such as bias toward mature workers, minorities, or women with small children. People will shut out great candidates because of their negative biases."

Brenda explains: "This [bias] has to come out in the selection process. A selection committee, as a whole, can be the conscience of the group. You want more than one person making a hiring decision if possible. You want other input based on the competencies for the role. And you don't want yes-men and -women on the selection committee, but people who are engaged that are going to speak up."

If left unchecked, bias can make its way into your own selection criteria by erecting barriers. For example, Brenda was conducting a board member search. The leaders said they wanted to select a woman to add diversity to the board. They selected a male with 30 years of experience instead of a well-qualified woman with 10 years of experience.

The issue was, at that time, no women had 30 years of experience on a board of directors. The board said one thing, "We want women on the board," but did another. Their own selection criteria had bias and barriers.

Next, I explored diversity, equity, and inclusion with Brenda, and she had wise insights to share. Hearing the phrase "diversity and inclusion" might cause one to think race and hiring quotas. We're talking about something else.

Brenda put it well when she said, "You've got to make sure that people have the same opportunities; equity recognizes that barriers do exist, and you have to look at your processes to see people sense equality. You might have to adjust, modify, or change in order to be inclusive. You need to understand how people are going to feel welcomed or valued."

She shared an excellent example to illustrate her point.

"I was in the middle of preparing for an academic search, and I had to give an overview on equity, diversity, and inclusion to the deans, PhDs, and academics on the selection committee.

"I'd been preparing for it, and I know this subject well. Here I am, on a call, and the client changed the technology. The young team that we have, they're millennials and Generation Xers, and they switched to a new program. So, I'm 63, and I'm on it [the technology], but I keep getting cut off.

"As I'm telling them about this inclusion piece, I'm telling them that what they've just done, by changing the technology and not giving me any training on it and just sending me to do this, that's not inclusive."

I thought that was a great example, that the younger associates took for granted participants were familiar with the technology. It's not that Brenda can't learn technology or wasn't willing to learn it. She wasn't given the opportunity and had to perform well in an important presentation while dealing with technology challenges.

Brenda emphasized that you can have diversity, which can be about different identities (race, gender, religion, nationality, sexual orientation) without being inclusive or equitable. Inclusiveness is having a sense of being valued, leveraged, and welcomed.

"You have to look at inclusion in terms of what the experience will be for the person coming in. Are there barriers standing in the way of people who are marginalized? And what's the impact on them? Are associates trained in differences, such as cultural training? We're not all the same. When you have diversity, you must have education or training on the uniqueness and differences in your organization. The onus is on the company and leaders to do that."

So, what? Now, what?

Brian, Greg, and Brenda all stressed the importance of a candidate having the right competencies and being a fit for the organization. Organizational fit usually comes down to temperament (such as character) and values. Early in my business, one of the services I offered clients was helping them discover the competencies needed for a role to help them write a job description. Following is the process I created to use with clients.

Hire Prework

Prior to identifying competencies for a role (for example, to support creation of a job description, succession planning, etc.) the following questions should be explored by significant stakeholders of the role. These questions accomplish at least three important things:

- They bring the greater context in view
- They cause differences in stakeholder expectations to surface
- They uncover overlooked factors such as culture challenges and future needs of the role

Ask three-to-five stakeholders to answer the following questions.

1. How will this position contribute to the team/department/company mission, vision, and goals?
2. What specific goals, deliverables, or expectations exist for this position now and possibly in the future?
3. What will differentiate a high performer in this role?
4. What challenges will they face?

All four questions are essential to ask, but the fourth one is rarely considered. Why is it that a candidate can have the perfect experience and interview well, yet ultimately end up being unsuccessful in the role?

Imagine you're a CFO and you hire an accountant who will be responsible for preparing the monthly invoices on a tight schedule with aggressive deadlines to bill clients. The person you hire has years of experience doing exactly what you need, including managing aggressive deadlines successfully. The cherry on top is you hit it off well in the interview.

Every month, the client invoices are sent late, and the accountant is defensive when you bring it up. You think he's making excuses, and you're frustrated because you've received complaints from operations about his attitude. Eventually, you end up parting ways with the associate.

What you might not have known is that 60 percent of the operations leaders who are responsible for submitting their reports to accounting in a timely manner to enable generation of client invoices aren't submitting their reports.

The accountant you hired was put in a position every month to follow up and exert influence over dozens of managers to motivate, coax, and persuade them to submit their reports. The monthly process became time-consuming and emotionally taxing for him, because he has no influencing strengths.

He is highly responsible, and the lack of accountability, consequences, or support of this situation began to erode his motivation and work satisfaction. In response, he became passive aggressive with operations leaders and defensive with you out of frustration.

The challenges within your organization's culture should not be ignored when considering fit. You'll find yourself reliving the experience with the next hire if your culture is creating barriers to associate success.

Aligned Values

In addition to the four questions, it's important to take into consideration the values of the team and organization to make certain the job description communicates the values sought in a candidate. Hiring managers should clearly outline the company's values by crafting behavioral interview questions to encourage candidates to demonstrate the expression of shared values in their work.

For example, if your team places a high value on personal accountability, you could prompt interviewees by saying, "Tell me about a time you took ownership for solving a problem you didn't create." If your team values curiosity and openness, say, "Tell me about a time you remained open to another person's point of view, which influenced a change in your thought process or course of action." If your culture is committed to inclusion, "Tell me about a time you were intentional to be inclusive of others who were different from you."

Once you've done the prework to gain clarity on the needs of the role and defined the values you're seeking in a new hire, you can begin the work to define the competencies needed for the role.

Competency, Defined

As you consider the requirements for a role, it's a good idea to filter decisions through a lens of diversity and inclusion and attempt to keep biases in the forefront of your mind. This can help avoid placing preferences in a job description that create barriers to entry.

An excellent example is the story Brenda shared about the board of directors requiring 30 years of experience when it was uncommon for women to serve on boards 30 years ago. That requirement creates a barrier that led to an all-male board. Ultimately, thought diversity is what we should strive for, and diversity of thought tends to occur among people who are different.

To define competencies needed for a role, ask the same stakeholders who answered the four questions in the prework to list skills and traits, with brief definitions, they believe are required for the role. After everyone has submitted their requirements, compile a master list with all suggested competencies. Add two columns for a vote to indicate if the skill or trait is a "must-have" or a "nice to have."

Distribute the complete list for stakeholders to indicate whether each competency is a must-have or a nice to have trait. Compile your results and select approximately 12 agreed upon "must-have" competencies to include in the job description. If you include too many requirements beyond twelve, you are treading into purple unicorn territory, and it will become more difficult to find candidates who meet a mile-long list of criteria. Stick to the most critical requirements, and you can always add the rest in a "nice to have" section on the job description. The direct manager can make a final call in situations where a decision is needed.

To illustrate, I created a sample list of requirements for a project coordinator role.

SKILL/ TRAIT	DEFINITION	MUST HAVE	NICE TO HAVE
Organize	Keeps work area neat, follows an orderly approach; keeps things organized	X	
Plan	Specifies steps for a project before beginning; prepares for potential problems before they occur	X	
Paperwork	Comfortable with repetition, attention to detail, maintaining accurate and timely records	X	
Manage Time	Able to use time wisely and productively to meet deadlines	X	

Manage Logistics	Manage events; handle detailed coordination of people, facilities, or supplies	X	
Customer Service	Assist, advise, solve customer problems, support customers appropriately	X	
Computer Skills	Use computers and related technology, such as Microsoft Office, efficiently, with a range of skills	X	
Collaborate	Willing to follow or lead, shows trust, supports coworkers; builds partnerships	X	
Ambiguity	Can act when details are unclear; comfortable leaving issues open; at ease with unknown		X
Change	Embrace or deal well with change to work priorities or focus	X	
Edit	Read or revise written or printed materials	X	
Write	Is concise, descriptive, and keeps readers in mind	X	
Research	Engage in data discovery such as conducting online research		X
Multi-task	Deal with more than one task or project at the same time		X

Interview Questions

Once you've finalized a list of competencies for the role, you can begin crafting your interview questions based on that list. Remember to include questions to assess fit with your team or organization's expressed values.

For example, in the above project coordinator role, I am looking to hire someone who can plan, manage time and paperwork, and handle logistics (in addition to eight other traits). I could add these to the job description and tailor them to my specific business needs, such as:

- Plan and create steps for an email and cold call marketing campaign to university MBA programs

- Track and maintain accurate records for prospect follow-up in Excel
- Effectively manage time and priorities across projects to reliably meet deadlines
- Manage logistics and handle detailed coordination of people, communications, and tasks for YouMap® certification training

After the job description is complete, I can craft interview questions tied to my requirements, as well as my values-based questions, such as this:

1. "Tell me about a project you've successfully managed that had tight deadlines and required coordination of people, communications, activity tracking, and regular status updates."
2. "Tell me about a time you've had multiple priorities to juggle and how you made sure deliverables were met across projects."
3. "Tell me about a marketing campaign you've planned, the steps you took, and the outcome of the campaign."
4. "Tell me about a time you took the initiative to learn new skills in the past six months." (I seek someone who values learning and growth.)
5. "Tell me about a time you demonstrated openness to understand someone else's point of view when you didn't agree with them." (I seek people who are flexible about being open to other opinions and not set in their ways.)

Now you're ready to begin selecting and interviewing candidates to assess fit with your requirements!

Final thoughts to consider when hiring:

1. Challenge unconscious bias by not counting out candidates such as those with career gaps, career changers, mature workers, and people who are different from you. Test yourself by asking, "So what?" when objections surface.
2. Remember, a person with ten years of experience could have one year of experience performed ten times. Years of experience does not

guarantee a person will be the best performer. Hire for attitude and aptitude. You can train skills; you can't easily train attitude.

3. Keep in mind, 85 percent of skills are transferable from job-to-job. Try to be open and look for transferable skills.

4. Remember, some people are performing burnout skills. They have the experience but might not enjoy performing those skills. Probe for a candidate's motivation to do the work during the interview process.

5. Two-thirds of the workforce are in a poor role fit. Past performance is not always a good predictor of future success. Don't assume a candidate won't be a good fit because their previous job titles aren't the same as the role you're hiring. What you are seeking might be exactly what they do best; career changers are often some of the best associates because they have heightened motivation upon leaving a poor role fit and finding a better one.

The next chapter, "Case Study: A Look at Role Fit," will introduce you to powerful insights on the nuances of getting the right people into the right roles through a powerful case study.

I will introduce you to the YouMap® profile, which is a holistic, intuitive, and actionable tool that uncovers a person's strengths, values, preferred skills, and personality-based career interests. It's helpful for hiring the right people in the right roles, professional development, team building, succession planning, and outplacement support.

CHAPTER 6

CASE STUDY: A LOOK AT ROLE FIT

"One of the most courageous things you can do is identify yourself, know who you are, what you believe in and where you want to go."

Sheila Murray Bethel, author and leadership expert

Get ready for several "aha" moments!

In this chapter, I share an actual client case study to illuminate the four pillars of career fit. Client names have been changed to protect the innocent. Before I dive in, I need to share a bit of context.

I was first certified as a career coach with my previous employer in 2007. Over the years, I chose to complete a half dozen certifications for assessment tools and used several other assessments that didn't require certification.

I always felt I was trying to piece and patch together tools to give a holistic view of associates and clients. As it turns out, other coaches and consultants felt the same way. When I couldn't find anything that satisfactorily displayed a simple, yet robust, view of clients, I decided to create my own. In 2017, I officially applied for the YouMap® copyright, though it was years in the making.

After speaking with approximately 2,000 associates, job seekers, and career changers, I saw a pattern. Four consistent themes contributed to a person's fit and satisfaction in a role: **strengths**, **values**, **preferred skills**, and personality-based **interests**.

The Four Pillars of Career Fit

Your Work Aligns with Your Strengths

Your strengths are your natural, innate talents. Everyone is born with natural talents, but not everyone realizes the talents they have or actively works to develop them. Regardless, people perform better when something is natural for them, whether building rapport with new customers, figuring out solutions to problems, mentoring people to reach their potential, communicating thoughts effortlessly, or learning new skills and information quickly.

The Gallup organization reports people who use their strengths every day in their job are up to six times more engaged at work than associates who do not use their strengths daily. They define engaged associates as spending at least 4.5 hours of their day so absorbed in their work that time passes quickly for them.[1]

Not only are people more engaged when they use their strengths, they're up to three times, or 300 percent, more likely to say they have a good quality of life, according to Gallup polls.[2]

Your Work Aligns with Your Values

A chief source of career misery I have encountered with clients is misalignment between one's work and values. Your values dictate what's most important to you.

According to Gallup's 2017 "State of the American Workplace" report, "The modern workforce knows what's important to them and isn't going to settle. Employees are willing to look and keep looking for a company whose mission and culture reflect and reinforce their values."

Because each person is distinct, values vary widely. Therefore, it's important to reflect on what's most important to you. Listening to the advice of others can be helpful but be cautious of values-based advice. People who value security will steer you away from bold or adventurous risks. Others who value wealth and status might encourage you to pursue a career because of the salary potential.

Your work must align with your values, not the values of your spouse, best friend, sister, or parents.

Your Work Aligns with Your Preferred Skills

Skills are the abilities and expertise which contribute to your capacity to perform competently in a role, and those skills are portable across many jobs. In fact, according to Korn Ferry International, 85 percent of skills are transferable from job to job. In my experience, many hiring managers don't realize how many skills transfer to a role. Transferable skills are not tied to a job or function and can be used across a variety of settings and industries.

Our interest in performing certain skills on the job are broken down to most preferred and least preferred skills.

Most Preferred Skills – Skills you're good at and enjoy doing every day or you're interested in developing. For example, you might love conceptualizing, managing processes, writing, dealing with ambiguity, or working with numbers.

Least Preferred Skills – Skills you're good at, or not good at, and do not enjoy doing. For example, you might be proficient at working with numbers but find it tedious and draining.

We should aim to spend a minimum of 80 percent of our day performing our preferred skills and 20 percent or less on least preferred burnout skills.

Your Work Aligns with How You're Wired

How you're wired refers to your natural preferences relative to interests, passion, and motivation. I often say "follow your passion" is misguided, though well-meaning, career advice because as you can see, passion is only one of the four pillars of career satisfaction. Therefore, the passion approach is too narrow to discover best career fit. Our career interests are heavily influenced by our personality.

Unique Contribution

Your unique contribution is a two-to-three-sentence summary of how your strengths, values, preferred skills, and personality-based interests contribute to the unique value you offer. In other words, defining/describing what you do best that others need most.

Danny's Story

I met Danny in mid-2018. He was a regional sales manager in his late thirties and had been in sales his entire career from medical device, pharmaceutical and laboratory sales to selling digital marketing services.

Early in his career, Danny participated in sales team building sessions where assessments were administered. He noticed he was often the only person with his personality type in the group, while the other sales representatives tended to be grouped together in other personality types. He thought it was notable but didn't think much more about it.

Danny told me he was unhappy in his job but couldn't pinpoint the core issue. He reported he felt tired at the end of the week and was struggling to stay motivated. One of the things he shared was, "You're only as good as your last quarter [sales]." Review the final summary page of Danny's YouMap® profile that follows, and I'll explain why sales is a poor fit and how Danny compensates.

PERSONALIZED YOUMAP® FOR:

DANNY DOWNER

How I'm Wired

A systematic thinker, planner, problem-solver, innovative, dynamic learner, methodical, analytical, efficient.

What I Value

Love/Connection, Purpose, Knowledge, Creativity, Achievement, Making a Difference, Health, Fitness, Safety, Security

My Strengths

Restorative, Intellection, Discipline, Futuristic, Learner

Skills I Enjoy

Analyze, Classify, Conceptualize, Perceive Intuitively, Generate Ideas, Plan & Organize, Visualize, Strategize, Read for Information, Research Online, Make Arrangements, Manage Time, Expedite, Implement, Test, Maintain Records, Write

My Unique Contribution

I quickly assess what's not working and solve problems creatively through inquiry, analysis, and pattern recognition. Leadership is a natural mantle: I provide the structure and direction for the team to reach its goals.

© 2018 YouMap LLC • All Rights Reserved
www.MyYouMap.com

YouMap® is a registered trademark of YouMap LLC.
Unauthorized use or reproduction of the YouMap® Career Profile is strictly prohibited.

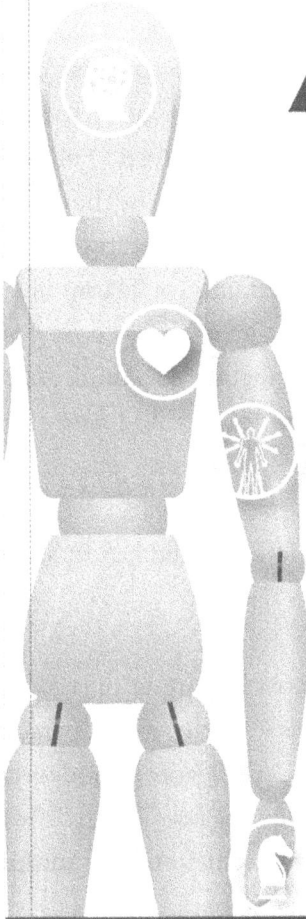

How Danny is Wired

"How I'm Wired" refers to a niche area of personality: career interest type. Danny's career interest type is known as "The Examiner," which means he is a *thinker* and an *organizer*. Danny's personality descriptors are: **systematic thinker, planner, problem-solver, innovative, dynamic learner, methodical, analytical, efficient**

When you think of a salesperson, are these the kinds of personality descriptors which come to mind for you? (No, me neither.) Right off the bat we can determine Danny's personality is atypical for sales.

When Danny first connected with a prospective client, he could think about the problems the prospective client had (problem-solver), get up to speed quickly on the customer's business and potential needs (dynamic learner) and plan and think through the solutions which solved the customer's problems (systematic thinker and planner, innovative, analytical). Danny used his thinking strengths to focus on the customer problem to find solutions, which was probably highly valued by customers.

Yet, the heavy people-focus in sales was draining for Danny. He was able to add value to customers, but it came with a great energy cost working so heavily with people and not having enough quiet time to think and plan. In addition, once the preliminary problems were solved and Danny learned the ins and outs of his customer, his thinking personality was no longer challenged as he maintained the account.

The bottom line: Danny's personality-based interests did not fit sales.

What Danny Values

Values are rarely examined but is one of the most important pillars. As you saw previously, Danny was able to compensate with other personality characteristics to survive in sales. Our values aren't accommodating; we break on our values, rather than bend. Following are Danny's values: **connection, purpose, knowledge, creativity, achievement, making a difference, health & fitness,** and **safety & security.**

Recall Danny's earlier comment. "You're only as good as your last quarter." Danny values safety and security, which includes financial security. He couldn't put his finger on it, but the competitive, prove yourself each quarter, nature of sales violated his need for safety and security. Danny is a husband and father; therefore, his perception of himself as a provider served only to exacerbate his unease.

Danny has purpose as a top value. While some people who are wired for sales would find deep purpose in this field, Danny was wired for a different kind of work. Therefore, sales did not fulfill his need for purpose. More importantly, connection to his family is his number one value, and he had to travel while working in sales. This was a major violation of what was most important to him.

Because Danny values achievement, he leveraged this value to meet his sales goals. Because many of Danny's values were violated, it is a pointless exercise to continue going through the rest of the list.

The bottom line: Danny's values are not honored in his sales role.

Danny's Strengths

Danny's natural talents are:

Restorative – The trouble shooter and problem-solver

Intellection – A deep thinker, wise, able to work alone

Discipline – An efficient organizer and planner; highly productive

Futuristic – Imaginative, creative, visionary

Learner – Always learning, catches on quickly, interested in many things

Notice the connection between Danny's strengths and the other two pillars ("How I'm Wired" and "Values"):

- **Creativity** is characteristic of the **Futuristic** strength. His **personality** is **innovative,** and he **values creativity**. Danny has congruence across his pillars of career fit.
- **Learner** is one of Danny's **strengths**. His **personality** is a **dynamic learner,** and he **values knowledge**.

(Is it just me or is this very cool?)

As with his personality, Danny was able to compensate in a sales role, because he is a planner and highly productive. His Discipline strength guaranteed he completed his tasks on time, which led to meeting his sales goals. In sales, it's far more common to see people with influencing strengths; the strengths which persuade and motivate others (to buy things). **The bottom line:** Danny's strengths were not ideally suited for sales and were being used in a compensatory way.

Danny's Preferred Skills

Our preferred skills are where the rubber meets the road. This is how we want to spend our day; what we want to be doing day in and day out.

Here are Danny's preferred skills: **analyze, classify, conceptualize, perceive intuitively, generate ideas, plan & organize, visualize, strategize, read for information, research online, make arrangements, manage time, expedite, implement, test, maintain records**, and **write**.

Now, I'm no rocket scientist, but that doesn't sound like a day in the life of a sales associate. But don't take my word for it. I captured the core required skills from a job description on Indeed.com for the role Danny was doing when I met him. I have highlighted the skills from the job description that are preferred on Danny's YouMap®:

Sell, including cold calling, negotiate, customer service, liaise, networking events, presentation skills

(Your eyes aren't playing tricks on you. No highlighting exists. Danny doesn't prefer any of the skills from the job description.)

The bottom line: Danny's preferred skill match for sales is a disaster.

Danny's Unique Contribution

We've established Danny isn't ideally oriented for sales and why he was able to compensate using other strengths, values, skills, and personality attributes. I would be inattentive if I didn't highlight what Danny does best.

Here is his "Unique Contribution Statement":

I quickly assess what's not working and solve problems creatively through inquiry, analysis, and pattern recognition. Leadership is a natural mantle: I provide the structure and direction for the team to reach its goals.

I don't know about you, but I think this is an extremely valuable contribution and something every organization needs. All organizations have problems, require solutions to those problems, and need a plan, process, and direction to implement the solution. This is what Danny does best that others need most.

Danny would be an excellent IT project manager. Imagine the gifts we throw away when we discard associates who are in a poor role fit.

Ellie's Story

Ellie is a corporate associate whose manager invested in her coaching as part of her professional development. She's currently an assistant controller in her company. Following is her YouMap® summary page.

PERSONALIZED YOUMAP® FOR:

ELLIE FOWLER

How I'm Wired

Systematic thinker, accurate, cautious, deeply engaged with whatever they do, quick with calculations, precise, uncompromising

What I Value

Inner Harmony, Trust, Wisdom, Compassion, Love/Connection, Making a difference, Generosity, Pleasure

My Strengths

Harmony, Input, Includer, Restorative, Analytical

Skills I Enjoy

Budget, Envision, Ideate, Innovate, Strategize, Collaborate, Use Intuition, Mentor, Motivate, Analyze, Observe, Research, Study, Delegate, Computer Skills, Numeric Accuracy

My Unique Contribution

Trust and consensus-builder who accepts and values others. A curious, resourceful and systematic thinker; enjoys analyzing and digging into problems to find reasons and causes to solve problems collaboratively and strategize solutions as part of a team.

© 2018 YouMap LLC • All Rights Reserved
www.MyYouMap.com
YouMap® is a registered trademark of YouMap LLC. Unauthorized use or reproduction of the YouMap® Career Profile is strictly prohibited.

How Ellie is Wired

Ellie has the same career type as Danny: "The Examiner." I chose to share her story to illustrate how different people can be even when they have the exact same personality type. No two YouMap® profiles are the same; even people who have a lot in common have very different needs, talents and preferences. Personality assessments alone (DiSC, MBTI, Insights) do not offer adequate insight to base career decisions or professional development because **personality is only one of the four pillars of career fit**.

Working in finance as an assistant controller is a good fit for Ellie. (I imagine Danny would fare better in finance over sales, too!) All the descriptors of "The Examiner," e.g., systematic thinker, planner, methodical, efficient, and analytical, are aligned with her role. Hooray!

What Ellie Values

Ellie's assessment uncovered the following values: **inner harmony**, **trust**, **wisdom**, **compassion**, **love/connection**, **making a difference**, **generosity**, **pleasure**

As we walked through and defined each of her values, we found all her values are honored in her current job and by her manager. Hooray, again! So far, Ellie is two for two on her four pillars of career fit. It's worth pointing out Danny and Ellie have only one value in common: making a difference. Values vary widely across people.

Ellie's Strengths

Things are about to get interesting! Ellie's natural talents are:

Harmony – Negotiator, can see both sides of a situation, great at asking questions, able to arrive at consensus, great facilitator

Input – Great resource, knowledgeable, excellent memory, mind for detail, collects interesting things, excellent conversationalist

Includer – Invites others in, caring, engages others, sensitive, takes up for others

Restorative – The trouble shooter and problem-solver

Analytical – Thinks things through, smart, logical, deep, thorough, comfortable with numbers, figures, and charts

Let's unpack this. Danny and Ellie are both "The Examiner," which means they are thinkers and organizers and possess the same personality descriptors as being methodical, accurate, precise people. Two very important insights:

1. Danny and Ellie have only **one** shared strength.

2. Ellie has two relationship-oriented strengths: Harmony and Includer.

It's easy to assume a person with a career type of "The Examiner," a thinker and organizer, is not a people-person. How many personality assessments ruled out candidates or passed someone over for promotion because of assumptions they wouldn't enjoy working with people? It cannot be overstated that natural talent heavily influences how a person works and what their priorities are. I always say you can't come between people and their strengths; you'll lose every time!

Ellie's Preferred Skills

The observations between Danny's and Ellie's skills are just as interesting as their strengths. They have only 38 percent of their preferred skills in common! Here are the seven preferred skills Danny and Ellie share in common:

research online, perceive intuitively, generate ideas, conceptualize, strategize, read for information, plan/organize, analyze

Ellie's skills below reveal she is good at and enjoys teamwork, motivating people, delegating, and mentoring. These are people skills! Remember, Ellie has the two relationship-oriented strengths **Harmony** and **Includer**, which influences the skills she's good at and enjoys. People are such fascinating puzzles, aren't they?

Ellie's preferred skills:

Teamwork, observe, research online, perceive intuitively, generate ideas, numbers (work with), innovate/invent, conceptualize, motivate, strategize, delegate, read for information, plan/organize, analyze, mentor, budget, synthesize, computer skills

Danny's preferred skills:

Analyze, classify, conceptualize, perceive intuitively, generate ideas, plan/organize, visualize, strategize, read for information, research online, make arrangements, manage time, expedite, implement, test, maintain records, write

Getting back to Ellie, the preferred skills pillar is where she has room for improvement in her career fit and satisfaction. Of Ellie's 18 preferred skills, she's using only nine. I figured this out by asking her which of her preferred skills she gets to use regularly in her role. That's using only 50 percent of her preferred skills on a regular basis. Remember, the goal is 80 percent.

I encouraged Ellie to speak with her manager when planning her stretch goals for the coming year to see where she can incorporate more of her preferred skills such as teamwork, innovate, and conceptualize. Perhaps she could take on a temporary process improvement project where she works with a special project team to develop and implement a needed business improvement. She loved the idea and planned to discuss it with her manager.

Ellie agreed she wanted to make a greater impact and become more useful (Recall making a difference is one of her values.), and she didn't feel she had enough teamwork in her role. This had been an area of dissatisfaction even though she is reasonably happy in her job. These small tweaks will make a measurable difference in her career satisfaction.

Ellie's Unique Contribution

I helped Ellie create her unique contribution statement by highlighting resonant words in her YouMap® and using them to generate a few sentences to explain her value to an organization.

Trust and consensus-builder who accepts and values others. A curious, resourceful and systematic thinker; enjoys analyzing and digging into problems to find reasons and causes to solve problems collaboratively and strategize solutions as part of a team.

As you can see from Ellie's unique contribution, she's in the right role–room for improvement exists, and YouMap® helped her pinpoint exactly what she needed that will align to a need in the business. A true win/win!

Tying it all Together

Now, a few takeaways. First, it's understandable when people are resistant to assessments. They believe they're being put into a box or labeled. It's not hard to see why, because assessments have a negative past. They were originally used to weed out "undesirables." The US military began using assessments almost 100 years ago to find soldiers who were apt to be affected by what we now know as PTSD, post-traumatic stress disorder, to reject them from service. Companies followed suit and began using assessments to weed out people. Ethically, I believe assessments should be instructive, not conclusive, and they should not be the sole basis for decisions.

Additionally, when administering assessments, many times we're looking at only one aspect of a person, which is over-simplified, because it doesn't take other factors into account. For example, we uncovered in this case study that two people with the same personality type are actually very different. Therefore, a holistic view of a person is needed, and we should approach assessments with a focus on celebrating people by valuing their differentiators and what makes them unique.

Another takeaway is not everyone has four out of the four pillars of career fit mismatched in a poor role fit. Some people have a great fit in their role for their strengths, preferred skills, and personality. When values are violated, it's an indication *where* the person is performing the role is the problem. It could be the way the role is performed in *that* organization, the manager the person reports to, or the organizational culture the person is working in.

Pinpointing where a breakdown is occurring is priceless information, because it becomes possible to make small tweaks to improve role fit and satisfaction, as in the case with Ellie. This knowledge is a win for the company, the manager, and the associate. In Danny's case, transitioning to a new role was the only workable solution.

What I want to emphasize here is we might write off associates as lazy, demotivated, or in worst cases, useless. What if an associate didn't have compensating strengths as Danny did? When people have available compensation strategies, they can get the job done, but they're not happy doing it, which is not sustainable in the long term.

When an associate doesn't have compensating strengths, they often end up on a performance improvement plan (PIP). My hope is now you can see why there's a chance this is not going to be effective when a person isn't wired for the work he or she is doing.

In cases where PIPs aren't going to work, we are just dooming the associate to "it's a matter of time before we get rid of you" instead of re-directing them into a role which fits them and enables them to be successful. It's not a matter of the person willing herself to have better performance. If she could, she would.

Getting people in the right roles is crucial because, as I've said before, you can't train or develop the wrong fit into the right one. Equally important to remember is a person who isn't performing well in one role could be a superstar in a different role. Wherever possible, find opportunities to move people who are in a poor role fit into another role which aligns with their four pillars of career fit.

Understanding your own pillars of career fit, as well as those of your team members, helps you understand why a person works and behaves the way they do. Suddenly, because we understand what *we* need to be satisfied at work, we develop compassion for how *others* need to work to be happy.

Our different workstyles aren't incompatible. When we're different, we fill in each other's gaps, and our bases are covered. Insights into who we are allow us to not only become more accepting of differences, but to embrace and value them. What a gift!

YouMap® profiles can be purchased for yourself, team members, or to evaluate candidate fit prior to making an offer at www.myyoumap.com/order-youmap-profile. You can find a YouMap® Coach for one-to-one coaching or a YouMap® workshop facilitator to work with your team at www.myyoumap.com/find-a-coach.

CHAPTER 7

ONBOARD: INTEGRATE ASSOCIATES

"Tell me and I forget, teach me and I may remember, involve me, and I'll learn."

Ben Franklin, founding father, United States

During my interview with Brian Ray for *Your Team Loves Mondays (…Right?)*, something Brian shared from his book, *Created for Good Works*, about onboarding resonated with me:

Onboarding is not only functional, it's personal. You start with building a relationship. You absolutely, positively, must touch that person every week on the topic of "How are you doing and what can we do to help?" And it doesn't have to be long. It can be 15 minutes, and that's fine. But if you don't connect on that level right off the bat, it becomes functional.

Most people in business think, "All I need to do is get the task done," and that's a huge mistake. To be effective and keep your people motivated, it must be functional *and* personal. In fact, most people miss this. It's all about relationships, but there are three kinds of relationships:

Positional – "I'm your boss."

Functional – "Here's what I do. Here's what you do."

Personal – "I'm really interested in helping you succeed. By the way, here are some things I need that would help me."

It might come as a surprise there is such a thing as formal onboarding. In speaking with people, I discovered it's common to confuse training and onboarding as the same thing, yet they are different.

Training is *teaching skills or knowledge* to improve productivity and performance.

Onboarding is a process of *integrating an associate* into an organization; not to assimilate, to unify.

Onboarding isn't just logistics, it's so much more!

This process of integration for new associates is crucial in setting them up for success. Have you ever joined an organization and felt they weren't expecting you when you arrived?

Have you had a new manager who didn't appear to have time to spend with you to orient you to your new role and organization? Have you ever felt like an afterthought to your new team? As if they were trying to figure out what to do with you on-the-fly?

If not, count your blessings. It feels lousy.

Nothing makes an associate question their decision to accept a job offer as a poor onboarding experience. Your new associate's enthusiasm is snuffed out at your own doing, even if unintentional.

In a global survey I conducted of 68 people managers, 88 percent of respondents said onboarding new associates is one of their greatest weaknesses.

I believe it.

In my own twenty-year career, prior to starting my own company, I've received a formal onboarding plan only once. It made such a big difference that I created onboarding plans for my new associates.

As a coach, I've heard too many onboarding horror stories. I was once coaching a woman who had just joined a new team. Several weeks into her new role, her badge still did not grant her access to the elevator, despite reminders to her manager. She had to wait in the lobby every time she needed to get on the elevator (first thing in the morning and after lunch) until another associate showed up so she could piggy-back up the elevator.

One of the worst onboarding stories I've ever heard was a woman who joined a new team at the same company. I spoke to her two weeks into her new position, and she reported no leaders, nor her new manager, had come to see her or spend time with her! I asked what she had been doing for two weeks, and she said she was trying to keep busy by reading and learning.

I asked if she had stopped by her manager's office or contacted her. She told me her manager's door was always closed, and she had received no response to her emails. Could this associate have been more assertive? Probably. But new associates should never be put in a position to have to advocate for their presence to be acknowledged. This is the responsibility of the manager.

Many managers are overloaded and often must do more with less. I get it, and I've been there. Attempting to attend to the important details of onboarding new associates so they believe they're valued and engaged becomes much easier with proactive planning.

Greg Brenner, whom I introduced in the hiring section of this book, agrees.

"How we receive someone into the organization is critical. If you invite someone to your house, do you expect them to just walk in and go to the refrigerator?

"You're going to welcome them. You're going to make sure you have all their needs met. You're going to introduce them to the people in the house. You're going to put out a drink, have snacks, and prepare all the necessities for their time with you.

"Do you have all the things in place that show them you knew they were coming? Or do they show up on the first day of work and they feel like you forgot they were coming?

"Onboarding is the continuation of the relationship that you built during the interview process. When you're recruiting, that's when the relationship begins. This is the next level up in your relationship. And you're going to put out the good china and put your best foot forward, but at the same time not put on a show.

"Onboarding is not about skill-building. You're teaching [new hires] about what it means to be an associate in this organization. It's understanding their needs throughout that timeframe. Onboarding is not one day. A relationship is not made in one day. It's a defined period where you're bringing a person up-to-speed, so they feel comfortable and they feel they have all the tools and know what to expect from the organization and know your management style.

"It's the most critical part, outside of the interview process, to building the relationship. First impressions are everything. If you treat a new hire terribly or if they're forgotten, they'll never forget that. You need to intentionally think about them before they get there and then provide continuous follow up after they arrive.

"By the time new hires get to you, onboarding shouldn't be about everything they can't do. It should be about what they can achieve there throughout their career. So, we do a global orientation, our history, what we value, what our service standards are, what we stand for, and how we treat each other. Everybody goes through orientation from CEO to plumbers.

"The next piece is what happens at the department level. That's where we tend to have a drop off. Your associate is not an HR responsibility. You're going to help them serve, develop, and grow. It's not someone else's role. You can't sublet your responsibility with your associates. It's not somebody else's job.

"When you get to the unit level, you're intentional about everything you do. Are you outside waiting for them? Do you want to wow them or treat them like they're just another person? You don't want your associate tracking you down. Do you put them with a buddy? It doesn't have to be lavish, but do you invite others to come meet the new associate and perhaps serve a simple snack?

"Set the schedule for what the next month or two is going to look like. What are they going to need to get up to speed on? Help them understand what's important as a team, what's the work we do and how do we fit into the bigger picture? Why do we do the work we're doing? It's important to connect on the emotional level and on the practical level (Where do I park?). What are some of the practical details they need to know?

"Overall, the word is intentionality. Understanding your role not only as the manager but also being very intentional on how you think through what your associate is going to need *before* they need it.

"If you think of the service industry, and I look at leadership as a service to others, you are automatically thinking about everything that you can control that is going to go well with this associate. You want to be intentional on what you can control."

For an onboarding perspective from outside an organization, I asked Brenda LaRose who, with more than 30 years in search and recruitment, has a plethora of experience helping clients onboard new managers and executives.

"I learnt over a decade ago that onboarding is key and significant to the success of the person. We developed an onboarding template that we use with clients to establish three to four key priorities that are realistic and achievable in the first year. Any more than that is too much. The average person, and I work with managers and leaders, takes 6.2 months to onboard where they are giving back more to the organization than they're taking. That's the average; some people can do it a bit quicker and some take a bit longer.

"Onboarding is where you're giving new hires information about priorities, who they're reporting to, what they need to do, introducing them to external stakeholders in the departments they're going to be interacting with, and providing strategic plans and any information even prior to them beginning once they sign the offer.

"A proper onboarding also means your new associates should be having check-ins with you or other people who are helping them onboard. Check-ins should occur a couple of times a week for the first month, weekly for the next few months, and every second week after that.

- How are you doing?
- Is everything going well?
- Are you getting the support that you need?
- Is there anything you need that I can help with?

"Also, depending on the organization, you want people helping with the onboarding that are positive associates, positive people who can contribute. You never want any person to help or mentor that's not upbeat or positive because they can poison them to the organization.

"Onboarding is so important because one-third of people will leave in the first 18 months because it's not what they thought, it's not what was promised, or they're not getting the proper onboarding, training, and development."

As Brenda shared, when you consider it takes 6.2 months, on average, for a new associate to make a significant contribution to the organization, an 18-month tenure is similar to one year of contribution. Considering the cost to recruit, onboard, and train associates, this sobering statistic should be a strong incentive to onboard effectively.

Following is a sample onboarding plan you can modify to suit the needs of your new hires. This is only an example. To create an effective onboarding process, I recommend the following steps:

1. Perform a mental walk-through of the people your associate will interact with, the systems they will access and the programs, products, or services they will be involved with. As you perform the walk-through, make a note of people they should meet, systems they will need access to and anything else they will need.
2. Solicit input from the team members who have most recently onboarded. Ask them what went well with their onboarding and what things were missed or any challenges they had.
3. Show the draft onboarding plan to one or two of your veteran high-performing team members who possess attention to detail or who are systematic thinkers for additional feedback.
4. Show a draft of your onboarding plan to other stakeholders whom your associate will serve or interact or collaborate with for a different take on what's missing, from their point of view.

Sample Onboarding Process

1. Decide onboarding **length** and **activities**, such as a three-to- four-week plan
2. Outline **key focus areas** for associate's first 60-90 days
3. Provide a **week-by-week** on-boarding overview

Create a basic outline for each week, including key individuals for relationship building related to the focus areas you outlined above. This could include team members, project team members, internal and external stakeholders, clients, customers, peers, and strategic partners. An onboarding outline might include:

- On-boarding task
- Purpose
- Meetings to schedule
- Responsible party
- Notes or info to review in advance of meeting

Set priorities for the first 60-90 days. For example:

- Establish leadership of team (coaching, development, work status)
- Ensure transition strategy (if applicable)
- Assess current state of key projects
- Include brief bullets of a "Beyond 90 Days" plan (Priorities can be set later.)

Sample Onboarding Plan

Week 1 Overview: Complete orientation, training, and meet team members

Task	Purpose	Meeting/Location	Responsible	Notes
New Hire Orientation	Onboarding	Mon – Wed 10am – 5pm Boone Conf. Rm	Xander	Lunch provided
Online Training	Complete new hire modules	At your desk train.onlineportal.com	Xander	Login: xsherry Pwd: P112301
Team Lunch	Meet the team	Thu 12:00pm – 1:00pm	Kristin	
Meet with Kristin	First weekly 1:1	TBD	Kristin	Bring any questions

Week 2 Overview: Knowledge transfer sessions for projects; system training

Task	Purpose	Meeting	Responsible	Notes
Meet Lori Knudsen	Knowledge transfer of Salesforce	TBD	Xander	6 hours
Train w/ Steve Sullivan	Azure Training	TBD	Steve	6 hours
KT with David Brier	KT of key client accounts	TBD	Xander	Schedule 2-1hr. KT sessions
KT with Justin Hedge	Key project updates	3/27 @11am	Justin	1 hour

Week 3 Overview: Meet key stakeholders, customers; process training

Task	Purpose	Meeting	Responsible	Notes
D&I Training	Culture Training w/ Cathy Bawden	3/31 Oak Conf Rm.	n/a	Full day
Set up ELT Meetings	Meet stakeholders on ELT	TDB	Kristin	1:1 with 10 ELT members
Manager Training	Required manager training	4/1-3	Kristin	3-day training

Week 4: Travel to customer site for strategy planning sessions

Task	Purpose	Meeting	Responsible	Notes
On-site w/ customer	Strategy planning for next fiscal year	Agenda to be sent	Kristin	Spend week at customer site

Key Priorities for first 90 Days

1. Establish strong relationships with team and stakeholders
2. Work through transition plan with David
3. Gain familiarity with project plan details for all assigned projects

Beyond 90 Days

1. Contribute to financial plan for Balanced Scorecard strategy
2. Lead system migration to Salesforce.com

The priority of your first meeting with your new associate should be getting to know him better. Another top priority for the first meeting is to go through the onboarding plan you created. Walk through the plan to ensure your new hire understands each item of the plan and give him a chance to ask clarifying questions.

CHAPTER 8

TRAIN: SET ASSOCIATES UP FOR SUCCESS

"The only thing worse than training your associates and having them leave is not training them and having them stay."

Henry Ford, American inventor

Prior to starting my coaching and training business, YouMap, LLC, I worked as a Learning & Development (L&D) leader in a Fortune 20 company.

I've read varying statistics and research on wasted training dollars, and they range from 75 percent to 90 percent.

The Association for Talent Development (ATD) reported a Western Michigan University study found just under 20 percent of learners never apply what they've learned in a training program back to their job, and an additional 65 percent try to apply what they've learned but return to their old way of doing things. In total, this equates to 80-85 percent in "scrap" or wasted learning.[1]

Greg Brenner shared his biggest challenge as a learning & development leader is how to bring the development to where the work is happening. For example, many managers don't know how to have difficult conversations or how to hold people accountable in a way that's not threatening. They might learn techniques in the classroom and then respond in the workplace in the way that's most natural to them instead of implementing what they learned in training.

Multiple factors contribute to the challenge of transferring training from the classroom to the job, but the top reason, according to senior training manager, Kimberly Tilley, is training isn't properly supported by leadership.

Kimberly, who has a master's degree in adult education and many years working in training at Fortune 100 companies, shared a very common scenario is senior leaders roll out major directional or policy changes, along with an expectation people will be trained in the new way of doing things.

When middle management doesn't buy into the change(s), it could be because they disagree, don't understand, are threatened by them, or a combination of these. This can manifest in how middle management treats the training expectation. They might deprioritize it but, more often, people go to the training and then return to their work to find change is not supported. Their manager might not set expectations to use new skills or knowledge, nor offer coaching to help the team member apply what they've learned. They might not expect—or even want—their team to apply what they've learned.

Culture must support training. In other words, training needs culture to succeed. Kimberly says, "Associates will prioritize what they see their leaders prioritize and ignore what leaders ignore. If leadership supports learning by participating in learning themselves, associates are going to place more value in expanding their own skills. On the other hand, if associates believe learning initiatives are merely going through the motions and are disconnected from the business, they're less likely to take it seriously."

When I was working in corporate, associates delivered a harsh evaluation of the management team's capabilities in an annual associate survey. In response, the organization created a mandatory management training program. The program was a mixed learning model of online classes and instructor-led training. All managers were expected to complete the entire training program within two years.

As a former L&D manager, I was responsible for learning delivery in the organization. One of the greatest challenges for my training team was cancellations and no-shows for the mandatory instructor-led manager training classes. The required training was automatically added to managers' transcripts in our learning portal. But there was no accountability or follow up.

Managers saw their leaders weren't taking the training, so they didn't either. It was common for my team to receive an email from registered participants saying they had work to do for a client and couldn't attend the training. It was common for people to not show up. Two years after the mandatory training was implemented, reports showed only one manager, in a company of 5,000 people, had completed the entire training program.

After associates complete training, even when they found it helpful and inspiring, a common barrier to organizations achieving a return on investment of their training dollars is associates return to the old way of doing things.[2]

When it comes to successful training initiatives, Kimberly's most effective strategy is to gain buy-in first, involving everyone who needs to have skin in the game. Kimberly says she typically holds an overview class before the required training for the team. Why?

"One reason managers don't help their teams apply what they've learned is because they don't understand what their team will be doing differently. It causes them anxiety to think their team may be doing something they don't understand. The best way to get them on board that I've found is to have an overview class before the actual training. I might say something like, 'You already know this information, but here's how I'm planning to break it down and explain it to your team.' By prefacing it this way, I can give the managers a high-level training to remove that anxiety they feel. They have the opportunity to ask questions they think 'people on the team' might ask. I can also talk to them about how they might coach to these new skills post-training."

Kimberly shared additional ways she mitigates resistance to training. "I think about what could be in it for the person and come up with creative ways to reward them for being part of the change. If there is a very resistant person who is continually throwing out objections, I put them in a key partnership role. 'I need you to help me figure this out as the most forward-looking person.' It motivates them to figure out the real problems. And I do my best to help them look good. I may mention to leadership that I've sought out this person to leverage their support."

Tips to Increase Training "Stickiness"

To increase the success of training, you should be pulling through the concepts regularly with your team.

- Use 15 minutes of your team meeting for storytelling
- Ask team members to share key learnings, best practices, and how it's helped them.
- Hold people accountable to apply what they've learned.
- Reward and recognize associates who adopt training on the job.
- Pair early adopters with slow-to-adopt associates for mentoring or job shadowing.
- Provide consistent coaching.

Greg Brenner advocates that training starts with you. You must model a spirit of learning, growth, and professional and personal development.

"First, understand where you are in your skill set and do what you need to do on your leadership development journey and have a plan in place on how your associates are going to get up to speed, as well. They need to be given enough knowledge to feel competent to get started. This is the next step in the relationship. You will help them have self-efficacy, believing they can do what they need to do."

Developing Team Training

In general, you should have two main areas of focus when considering your core team training: process training and reskilling. Your core process trainings are the requirements for the associate to do their job effectively, such as customer service training and systems training.

Reskilling is needed when changes are made, such as modifications to procedures, new software implementations, or changes to the role itself.

Your training team should help you find your training needs by conducting a needs analysis with you, which should include tests to measure associate knowledge and effectiveness of the training. If you work in a small organization that doesn't have a formal training team of instructional designers, these seven steps will give you a starting point:

1. **Decide desired business outcomes** – Define what success looks like. How would you measure the outcome?
2. **Link desired business outcomes with associate behavior** – What behaviors are needed in associates to produce the business outcomes?
3. **Identify trainable skills/competencies** – What skills or competencies must the associates be trained in to reach the desired behavior?
4. **Evaluate competencies** – Assess your associates' skill level for each competency.
5. **Find performance gaps** – Identify training opportunities for your associates where performance needs improvement.
6. **Prioritize training needs** – Assess priority of training from most to least important.
7. **Determine how to train** – Choose the most appropriate learning modality for the competency to be developed.

It's important to integrate multiple learning styles and mixed modes of learning into your training efforts. Mixed modes could include on-the-job practice, video modules, assigned reading, online eLearning modules, job shadowing, and instructor-led training.

The Seven Learning Styles

The reason we need different learning modalities is because people learn differently. It's easier to retain the learner's attention when you leverage mixed-modal training. The following learning styles are based on Gardner's Theory of Multiple Intelligences.

Visual (spatial): Prefer using pictures, images, and spatial understanding
Aural (auditory-musical): Prefer using sound and music
Verbal (linguistic): Prefer using words, both in speech and writing

Physical (kinesthetic): Prefer using one's body, hands, and sense of touch
Logical (mathematical): Prefer using logic, reasoning, and systems
Social (interpersonal): Prefer to learn in groups or with other people
Solitary (intrapersonal): Prefer to work alone and use self-study

The most effective training modules will incorporate as many learning styles as possible. For example, if you're creating a customer service training for a new hire, your customer service training program could include an instructor-led class for role play and hands-on practice, with an eLearning component that contains a visual presentation, along with transcribed text, downloads for further reading, and optional audio support. This allows learners to read the training copy, listen to it, and view graphical representations of the content.

Your training program should include a training schedule, including how often you need to retrain or reskill your associates. In the next chapter, I go in depth to give you a comprehensive, yet simple, process for associate development.

Chapter 9

Develop: Maximize Potential

"Your value will be not what you know; it will be what you share."
Ginni Rometty, CEO, IBM

Your greatest value as a manager is to facilitate the success of your people. Too often, high-performing individual contributors are promoted to management and continue to perform as individual contributors with direct reports.

In other words, the new manager tends to focus efforts on her new individual tasks such as running reports, going to meetings, talking with clients, and the day-to-day execution she's responsible for, not seeing proactive direction of the team as her primary objective. Often, the team can be viewed as an interruption to getting other tasks done.

You might have said it yourself, "I don't have time to get my work done, let alone develop my team! I get frequent interruptions from team members asking questions or coming to me with problems where they need my help."

My response to these kinds of statements is, **"Your team is your number one responsibility."** If your team is not successful, you won't be successful. Their combined effort contributes more toward organizational results than any individual manager. That doesn't mean your contribution isn't valuable. It is!

The body of research is vast on productivity gains when managers invest time and effort into their associates. In the chapter, "Associate Demotivation: 7 Causes" I share a statistic that motivated associates are 31 percent more productive. Ignored associates are not going to experience an increase in motivation.

Second, if your team is continually bringing you questions and problems, you haven't empowered them. If you're fielding a lot of questions, your team is dealing with process gaps and lack of clarity. Additionally, associates must be coached and empowered to solve problems. Yes, there are complex issues where a manager must intervene. Yet, routine questions and problems become a reflexive habit when a manager hands down answers instead of using coaching conversations to help team members build self-sufficiency.

When a team member presents you with a routine question or problem, try the following:

1. Listen. Resist the urge to give an answer.
2. Ask questions with a curious, but not accusatory, tone.

- What are you trying to achieve?
- What resources could help you with that?
- How might you get what you need to achieve it?
- What could you try to make that happen?

Answers to these questions might help you see the areas where your team is struggling with current processes perhaps you weren't aware of, which will assist with process improvement. If you offer answers, those process gaps are never closed. By closing your process gaps, you create clarity for your team and equip them to find their own answers to common questions. This requires you to intervene only in tricky or one-off situations. Asking these questions retrains your associates to first attempt to solve a problem without contacting you purely out of habit.

Once the team's questions and problems decrease, you will have more time to intentionally invest in your team's success. You might still be thinking you don't have time to develop your people, so I'll address this a bit further before we move on to developing your associates.

As mentioned previously, I once led a team of 31 direct reports, so I understand the idea of developing a team of people is overwhelming and perhaps seems unrealistic. And it would be, if you believe you own the process.

Remember:

Associates own their careers.

Managers should give support.

Companies should provide resources.

It's not your responsibility to manage the careers of your direct reports. You are *supporting* their development and providing guidance for *them* to take action. Resist the temptation to own the process; allow them to drive with you guiding from the side.

Not all associates are going to take you up on your offer to support them through a development process. Some associates will undertake their development independently, while others won't prioritize their development. The Pareto principle (known as the 80/20 rule or the law of the vital few) states roughly 80 percent of the effects come from 20 percent of the causes. As it relates to your associates, 80 percent of your time is spent on 20 percent of your staff. For example, 80 percent of time dealing with performance problems is spent with 20 percent of associates.

The Pareto principle holds true with development as well. When I offered to help 26 people on my team create formal development plans, only three associates took me up on my offer. Interestingly, all three of those associates went on to significant promotions in their careers! People get caught up in the urgent, immediate demands of their day and, therefore, commit less time to address the non-urgent but important activities of self-development.

If you truly don't have time in your week to invest in associate development, discuss your priorities and workload with your manager to avoid taking on too many responsibilities which keep you from supporting your team.

To summarize:

1. Supporting associate development is not as daunting as it seems. You should already be having regular one-on-one meetings with your direct reports as a matter of course. If not, it's not too late to start and structure your conversations to incorporate development.

2. The Pareto principle dictates not all associates are going to engage in a development process, despite your offer of support.

I think I might have heard you say, "What if my company is focused on metrics and the bottom line instead of developing people?" Develop them anyway. When I first started managing the team mentioned previously, my immediate manager came to me and said, "You need to drive your team for results. You need to stay on them."

I told her that wasn't my management style, and I made her a deal to let me manage the team my way and, if we didn't get results, I would try it her way. My team met their goals every month of the two years I managed them without me staying on top of them.

Kay Wakeham, Global Vice President of Talent at Citi, offers this advice, "Working to support both the individual and the team members, as a system, will free you to think strategically about the business, learn yourself, and continue developing your high-performance team."

Now, let's move on to the nuts and bolts of a process to support your staff with their development.

Some organizations offer formal Individualized Development Plans (IDPs) for use by their associates. The best IDPs are simple. Complex documents will deter people from using them—especially people for whom administrative tasks are a burnout skill! A simple tool that's easy to use will always outdo a complex document no one opens.

An IDP doesn't need to be complicated. If your organization doesn't mandate use of a company IDP template or doesn't have one, I will help you create a simple document for your associates using a spreadsheet, such as Microsoft Excel, or a word processing document, such as Microsoft Word. All it takes is a few simple steps.

Following is a high-level, four-step process you could introduce to your team to help them have a sense of vision for their career and take the steps needed to bring the vision to reality. Each of these four steps will be broken down in detail with guidance to execute each.

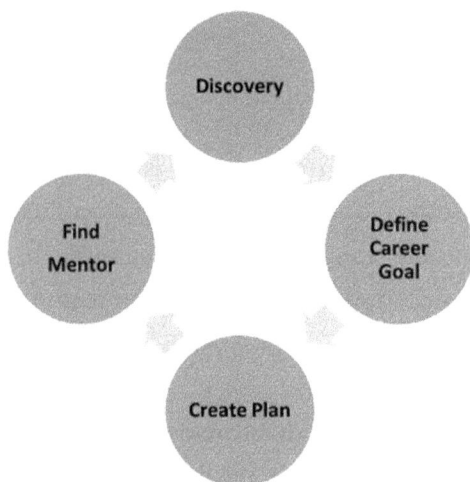

Step 1: Discovery
It's hard to read the label when you're inside the jar. Help your associate find her four pillars of career fit to ensure her career vision aligns with what she does best and values most. The four pillars of career fit are:

a. Strengths
b. Values (what's most important to her)
c. Preferred Skills (skills she performs well and enjoys using)
d. Career Interests

See the chapter titled "Case Study: A Look at Role Fit" to learn more regarding the four pillars of career satisfaction.

Step 2: Define Career Goal

Discuss possible options within the organization based on the outcome of step one, "Discovery." Here are questions to consider and work through with your team member:

a. Where is the organization growing?
b. What skills would she need to leverage?
c. What capabilities does she need to build?
d. What opportunities fit her needs?
e. What are her development options?

Step 3: Create Plan
There are two steps to creating a development plan.
First, identify the specific skills to develop. Find gaps between associate's current capabilities and required future capabilities for the career goal defined in step two.

Second, create an action plan.
List competency/skill to build, define the current state, what the desired future state should look like, and development actions to take.

Step 4: Find a Mentor
Encourage/support your associate to find a mentor to support development.
As a rule, it's a conflict of interest for a direct manager to serve as a formal mentor. Associates should be free to discuss all challenges and obstacles with their mentor; sometimes those challenges are the manager.

Finding a Mentor
Managers can serve to expand the network of their associates by introducing them to potential mentors. You can support your associate by helping them understand the roles and expectations within a mentoring relationship, especially if she hasn't participated in this type of relationship before.

The responsibilities of a mentor are:

Advisor: Recommend direction, identify obstacles, assist in overcoming

Ally: Offer candid, forthright opinions

Broker: Assist in establishing and increasing network contacts

Catalyst: Promote understanding of organizational culture and clarify employer expectations

Communicator: Facilitate discussion, interaction, and the exchange of information

The responsibilities of a mentee (the person being mentored) are:

- Fully engage in the relationship
- Be open to constructive feedback
- Set meetings and agendas
- Show up on time and be prepared for scheduled meetings
- Follow up on action items
- Identify and track goals
- Align key learnings from mentor with own situation

Before we explore the development planning framework I created when coaching emerging leaders, let's review the accepted best practice for executing a development plan. Keep this top of mind as you support your associates in creating their plan. Implementation of a development plan should follow a 70/20/10 ratio:

- 70 percent of development is achieved through on-the-job skill building.
- 20 percent of development is achieved through mentoring relationships.
- 10 percent of development is achieved through formal training such as courses, workshops, and conferences.

ROI studies on training and development clearly show development efforts which emphasize application on the job yield the greatest results.

Now, let's dive into the development planning process!

Development Planning Best Practices

The following list contains 10 best practices you can share with associates to help them increase the success of their development plans.

1. **Be selective** – Decide critical skills you need to develop based on stated career goals. Set reasonable goals you can accomplish in a realistic timeframe.
2. **Ask for detailed feedback** – Seek behavioral feedback on your development needs from others you work with. Ask questions to get specific examples. When? Where? With whom? In what situations? How often?
3. **Identify what you need to start, stop, and continue doing.**
4. **Learn from mentors** – Find several mentors who excel in one area you want to grow instead of trying to find one person who has everything. Reduce what they do (and don't do) to a set of practices to incorporate into your behavior.
5. **Read books covering your needed area of development** – What are how-tos of the skill? How is the skill best learned?
6. **Read biographies** – Learn from people who have the skill you want to build.
7. **Learn from a course** – Choose a course that gives a chance to practice the skill.
8. **Take on a stretch task** – Seventy percent of skill development occurs on the job. Track the positive and negative aspects of your performance and note everything you want to do differently or better next time.
9. **Track improvements** – Set goals for yourself and celebrate as you reach milestones. For example, if you're working on approachability, set a goal to initiate a conversation with five new people weekly.
10. **Get regular feedback** – Ask both people who know you well and those who haven't known you long, to gain different points of view.

Development Planning Worksheet

Following is a simple worksheet I created in Excel to help associates clarify development needs for their career. The worksheet captures the responsibilities of a target opportunity, the key strengths and skills the new role or opportunity requires, and any suggested development resources provided by a mentor. In the example, I include the ability to track current and potential next roles to support a long-term career vision.

Current Role/Next Role	Key Required Strengths/Skills	Mentor Recommended Experiences/Resources
Current Role - Summary of responsibilities/oversight	Based on current expectations and defined responsibilities	e.g. Side-by-sides, mentor, skill-based mentoring, on-the-job stretch tasks
Next Role - Summary of responsibilities/oversight	Based on research/discussion with someone in relevant role	e.g. Side-by-sides, mentor, skill-based mentoring, on-the-job stretch tasks

After pinpointing competencies to develop, the next step is to create an **action plan**. The associate should refer to the "Development Planning Worksheet" and the "Development Planning Best Practices" list on the previous pages to build an action plan. This is something your team member can do with input from you and/or a mentor.

Building an Action Plan
5-Step Action Plan for Competency Development

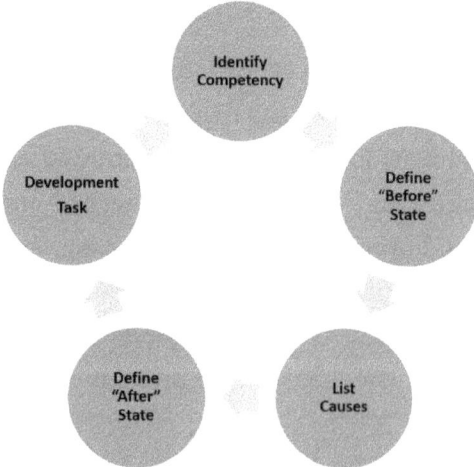

I will review each of the five steps to clarify how to build an action plan, but first, examine the image below of a simple action plan for visual learners that offers context as I discuss each step of the plan.

COMPETENCY	BEFORE STATE	CAUSES	AFTER STATE	DEVELOPMENT TASK	NEXT STEPS
Enter each competency to develop in this column	How would you describe yourself as it relates to this skill, currently?	What causes might explain your current skill level in this competency? For example, if you're not skilled in delegating, is it because you aren't familiar with delegation best practices or do you have difficulty letting go of tasks?	What would you like this competency to look like in you **after** you've increased your effectiveness in this skill?	What are some development tasks that will lead to the desired after state?	List any actions to take.
Delegate	I have trouble delegating. I worry the task won't be done right.	I struggle with perfectionism and I can be critical of other people's lack of attention to detail.	I'd like to be able to let go of my unrealistic standards and trust others to take on some of the tasks that have become routine for me.	I plan to discuss my perfectionism with my mentor for advice and then identify a task and delegate to a team member whom I trust and who is well-suited for the task.	Schedule meeting with my mentor for next week to discuss.

Step 1: Identify Competency
This step should be completed first by working through "The Development Planning Worksheet" introduced previously. Once the competencies for development have been selected, enter them in the first column of the action plan. In the above example, delegation is a skill the associate chose to develop. The remaining steps, two through five, are completed within the action plan.

Step 2: Define "Before" State
This often-overlooked step is critical. Once the team member identifies a list of competencies, the associate, with your support, should assess and characterize their current performance level for each skill. This step is important because it helps find the appropriate level of development and support needed.

For example, if the associate has no experience, formal training might be needed, followed by an on-the-job skill-building project. If the associate performs the skill moderately well, pairing the associate with a job coach or associate with a high level of skill in this area might be enough.

Step 3: List Causes
This step tends to be overlooked in development planning. It's important to list any possible causes affecting the current skill level. In the action plan

example of delegation, multiple reasons might contribute to someone not delegating well.

For example, an associate who mistrusts others to perform to his standard requires a different development strategy from someone who hasn't delegated. A person who has never delegated might not realize he shouldn't closely manage how the task is completed or that he needs to create a clear picture of the results expected and be available to support the person. An e-learning course on delegation could potentially offer the knowledge needed to achieve effective delegation.

Step 4: Define "After" State
In this step, the associate should outline what his performance should become as a result of his development efforts. It's difficult to measure if development was a success without defining the desired performance outcomes first.

For example, if a team member wants to improve presentation skills in meetings, the after state could include measurable improvements such as eliminating common filler words such as, "um," or "you know," and "like" to increase professionalism and decrease distraction for the audience.

Step 5: Development Task
In this step, the associate outlines each step he will take to improve his skill for each competency. Again, if the causes are not listed in the action plan, the development tasks could fail to address all causes affecting performance.

A bonus sixth step, "Next Steps," was added to the action plan to increase accountability between the associate, you, and his mentor. A plan without defined next steps is easier to neglect. Encourage your team members to set weekly goals and celebrate accomplishments.

One final thought on development planning is hooking the above activities into an existing process, such as your organization's performance review process. If you hinge on something you're already doing—a pre-established habit—it's far more probable the development plan will stick.

Another way to create and maintain momentum on your team's development is to incorporate development plan discussions into a scheduled weekly, twice monthly, or monthly meeting. Include an agenda item to ensure ongoing development discussions.

I often use a tool my mother and executive coach, Judi Spear, created called "The 5 Questions." Try incorporating these questions into your one-on-one meetings with your direct reports.

What's working?

This question is designed to surface the benefits and positives of your associate's development progress. How can you leverage or expand on her progress?

What needs to be done better or differently?

This question introduces the need for change in a nonthreatening way that opens people to possibilities. It is future-focused. By looking across the suggestions, begin to think about what the changes have in common so they can be grouped, then focus on the critical few.

What's preventing improvement?

This question is designed to surface barriers to the changes. Again, look at what the barriers have in common, focusing on the critical few. This is a good time to ask about possible obstacles that might impede progress on the things that need to be done better or differently.

If you could make one change, what would it be?

This question can bring a strong focus on the most important change that needs to be made. Is this the best place to start?

How can I help?

Asking people how they might help accomplishes two things:

1. She might recognize she is the barrier to improvement, and something about her behavior or attitude needs to change.

2. You can develop a resource inventory based on skills, talent, knowledge, experience, etc., in the group to best assign staff projects.

These five questions give you, the manager, an opportunity to weigh in on what's going well, what needs to improve, barriers you observe, what you think the highest priority change is, and how you can help your associate. It's a nonthreatening way to share feedback, which you should continuously offer during one-on-one sessions.

The Importance of Feedback in Development

Development consists of more than supporting and guiding the career of your associates through on-the-job skill building and opportunities for formal and informal training. A crucial part of the development process is consistently providing feedback on an ongoing basis, which includes recognition as well as constructive feedback.

Building a feedback culture requires regular touch points with your associates. Unfavorable feedback at performance review time should never come as a surprise. I have a colleague who was told at her mid-year performance check in she was exceeding expectations. At the end of the year she was stunned to discover she was given a "does not meet expectations" on her annual performance review.

Her manager did not initiate a single conversation about her performance after the mid-year evaluation when she was told she was exceeding expectations. This resulted in losing her annual bonus and the ability to apply for internal promotions. If her manager had shared performance concerns, my colleague could have course corrected. At review time, this feedback comes too late, which is unfair to the associate.

Offering constructive feedback, candidly and with compassion, is a skill requiring practice. If you aren't intentional about increasing your feedback skills, you could end up dancing around the subject, being too blunt or harsh, becoming defensive, offering subjective opinions without concrete examples, profusely praising without addressing needed growth areas, or avoiding difficult conversations.

Previously, I introduced you to Lila Smith in the "Characteristics of Effective Managers" chapter. Part of Lila's work involves helping people "verb" their values. She helps people discover their three values in verb form so they can learn to live out these verbs with intention in their communication with others.

Lila shares an important clarification about communicating with compassion.

"Giving feedback in a compassionate manner is great, as long as the compassion is communicated through intention rather than confusion. Managers who want to be liked will make their message unclear by drowning the point in apologetic language.

"If the issue is that an associate is not collaborating with a coworker, and therefore deadlines are getting missed, here's the content to communicate:

- Expectations
- Performance
- Challenges
- Strategies

"And here's what you might hear: 'I know you don't get along with Adam, as he can be very blunt sometimes. I know that hurts your feelings and makes it hard for you to want to work with him. But could you and Adam please find a way to get along? I'm sorry to have to ask, but we really need the team spirit here to grow.'

"The message about expectations and performance is buried, and there's no actionable guidance.

"Let's try again with content plus the intentions of to uphold, to mentor, to empower.

"'This week's deadline was missed. I needed you to collaborate with Adam on this. I know you prefer to work with Chet because he's fun, but Adam is our subject matter expert on this. He's really driven by performance indicators rather than relationships, so try to be a partner to him and communicate around your shared goals this week.'"

Think about feedback you've given. Do you consider your objective before you have the conversation? What about setting intentions to make sure what you say leads to achieving your objectives? Do you consider the objectives and what's important to the person to whom you're delivering feedback?

If you need additional help with delivering feedback, revisit the section on Emotional Intelligence in the "Discover Your Management Style" chapter and in the chapter below, "Retain: Value Your Treasure" under "Offer praise. And negative feedback."

CHAPTER *10*

RETAIN: VALUE YOUR TREASURE

"People are definitely a company's greatest asset. It doesn't make any difference whether the product is cars or cosmetics. A company is only as good as the people it keeps."

Mary Kay Ash, entrepreneur

Keeping your best associates doesn't mean holding them hostage.

In my interview with Greg Brenner, he addressed the issue of managers clinging too tightly to associates.

"You don't own anybody. You don't own their career. Our role is to hire, onboard, train them up, and then help the person navigate their career. They may stay with you and have a 20-year career and that's great, or they may want to do other things. You'll be a hero leader if you have people who grow and expand. Check your ego and understand your role is to help others grow, and if you're blocking your associates, it's a failure in your leadership."

Ouch! That's necessary tough love. When I was coaching 10 high-potential associates for a Fortune 100 client, a participant brought to my attention something that bothered me. One of my former direct reports applied to the program that prepared high-potential individual contributors to become managers in the company. Her current manager gave feedback to the program she didn't think her direct report was cut out for management. When this feedback was shared with the program applicant, she approached her manager and asked what led her to this conclusion. Her manager replied, "I need you on the team. I can't afford to lose you."

Well, guess what? That associate felt so betrayed she brushed up her resume and left the company. A high-potential, top performer found a new opportunity working for a competitor. Blocking advancement of an associate will almost certainly guarantee you lose them as well as your credibility.

Gallup's "State of the American Workplace Report," reported, "Employees who are engaged are more likely to stay with their organization, reducing overall turnover and the costs associated with it. They sense a stronger bond to their organization's mission and purpose, making them more effective brand ambassadors. They build stronger relationships with customers, helping their company increase sales and profitability."[1]

Research tells us increasing associate engagement is a solid strategy to reduce turnover and retain associates but how, exactly, do you increase engagement on your team? First, I would be remiss if I didn't refer you back to the "Associate Demotivation: 7 Causes" chapter. This is a good place to start reflecting on your team and where you need to make improvements.

I encourage you to take time now to work through the steps in the "Develop: Maximize Potential" chapter and, if applicable, work with your own manager to create an individualized development plan. The feedback step can help you target areas to improve.

To recap, the seven causes of associate demotivation are:

1. Lack of flexibility
2. Short-term objectives with no career vision
3. Feeling undervalued
4. No development opportunities
5. Poor leadership
6. Conflict
7. Unrealistic workload

Following are additional tips to increase engagement.

Look out for good work

It's a natural human tendency to pay attention to what's wrong and overlook what's working as expected. Managers must train themselves to be on the lookout, daily, to find associates doing good. And when you catch associates doing good, let them know. Create a habit of doing this and you'll ensure No. 3 on the "Associate Demotivation" list, feeling undervalued, doesn't happen on your team.

Promote autonomy

Micromanagement is one of the top complaints associates have about their managers. Health coach and personal trainer, Char Aukland, shared with me one thing she wants managers to understand is associates are not merely extensions of them. "I feel that treating people as autonomous and intelligent promotes a sense of self-efficacy that will help ensure better performance. However, micromanaging fosters bitterness and resentment."

How can you promote autonomy?
- Delegate tasks instead of doing everything yourself.
- Set clear expectations for results; allow freedom on how to achieve it.
- Keep a big-picture focus instead of homing in on correcting details.
- Allow team members to make decisions; consult them on decisions.
- Resist taking back a project if a mistake is made; coach and support.

Encourage openness

Approachability is foundational to trust. Not only do associates need to know they can approach you, they need to know you are open to their ideas, input, and feedback. In addition, associates will be more willing to keep you informed, which will help you find out about mistakes earlier and be more "in the know." Tips to increase approachability include:

- Keep your door open unless you're in a meeting. Set your desk up to face your door.
- Don't respond defensively or make excuses in response to feedback.
- Smile and respond in a welcoming manner when approached.
- Use relaxed, open body language.
- Say thank you.

Admit your mistakes

Being the manager doesn't mean you have to know everything and you're perfect. That's unrealistic and futile. If you could do everything, and do it perfectly, you wouldn't need a team! People respect someone who can admit their mistakes. And remember, people already know when you've made a mistake, and they even know what your weaknesses are—it's not a secret.

Lindy Chapman, a relocation strategist, shared with me she dealt with active opposition and lack of support toward not only her but others she worked with. She adds, "The best managers are those who can admit they don't know everything and are willing to see the strengths of their team as a complement to their areas of weakness. When a manager delegates and develops the strengths of those they lead rather than feel threatened, that's a sign of truly great leadership that creates a culture of trust and purpose allowing a team to thrive."

Share the spotlight

Bob Sager, founder of SpearPoint Solutions, helps organizations increase their innovation capabilities. Bob told me one of the top reasons associates won't share ideas with their manager is too many managers will take credit.

The best manager I've ever had, Laura Casoni, not only didn't steal ideas I shared, she invited me to present my ideas. I've never forgotten it, and her support garnered my loyalty and respect. On the other hand, I've shared an idea, and my manager presented it without telling me. I remember exactly how it made me feel too.

Having an abundant mindset is necessary to be a successful manager. Scarcity mindset will tell you someone else's good idea will take from your success. That's nonsense. Another person's success never precludes your success, because ideas and innovation are not a resource; therefore, they are available in abundance.

Our egos can give us bad advice, "Hey, you better take credit for the idea, because your associate is going to look smarter than you, and it's going to make you look bad." Who said the manager needs to be the smartest or have the most ideas on the team? It's okay if someone has a higher IQ than you do or is a natural idea machine.

Understand what you do best, work those strengths, and you, too, will shine. If you're doing your job and helping your team excel in their own gifting, when the time is right, your associates will get promoted somewhere else in the company or will leave the company for a new opportunity. Their success will never make you look bad. But you know what will? Stealing credit.

Be supportive

There are many times when your associate might need your support. This includes everything from going through a family crisis to struggling to learn a challenging new skill. Supporting people doesn't need to be complicated. It comes down to two simple things:

1. Demonstrate you care through your words and actions.
2. Ask, "What can I do to best support you?"

That's it! Show you care and ask how you can best support them. Showing you care can be as simple as asking them about how things are going with a situation. It shows your team member what they're dealing with isn't off your radar. Offering your support is an invitation to clear roadblocks, offer additional resources, etc. If you make these two things a habit, your consideration will go a long way.

Treat people fairly

A manager playing favorites is a sure way to damage credibility. Many times, managers do this without realizing it. It's true some associates are easier to like than others; they work harder and have better attitudes and congenial personalities. Regardless, it's important to keep favoritism on your radar and off your team—it's a culture killer. Here are some ways to guard against favoritism:

- Use objective measures to rate performance instead of subjective performance ratings.
- Apply policies equally across associates; don't make exceptions for one associate while writing up another.
- Spend equal amounts of time with your direct reports.
- Avoid crossing boundaries, such as having lunch with your favorite associates.
- Avoid favoritism in hiring and promotion decisions.
- Avoid cutting off praise to associates who are harder for you to connect with.

Address conflict

Seventy percent of people fail to report bad behavior witnessed at work instead of speaking up.[4] This is not an option for a manager who doesn't want his team eaten from the inside out like a house with a termite infestation.

Conflict not only affects the individuals involved; it spreads demotivation to team members who are exposed to the conflict around them, increasing sick days and decreasing productivity. Here are some steps to manage conflict among team members:

1. Acknowledge the issue with the parties involved.
2. Share the effect the conflict is having on the team.
3. Gain agreement to openly discuss the conflict.
4. Set expectations: no insults, assumptions or interpretations. Make fact-based observations only.
5. Help each person clarify their position while the other actively listens.
6. Build agreement, then decide a course of action. Who is going to do what? By when?

Be open to feedback

Feedback is tough for most of us, especially when poorly delivered. It's essential to be open to how we're perceived by others. Feedback is a gift because it gives us an opportunity to do better and be better. One of my favorite sayings is, "Eat the meat, spit out the bones." Even if feedback is delivered in a critical manner, there is still "meat" we can consume, process, and incorporate into our growth. Lila Smith shared how to do this during her interview in the "Characteristics of Effective Managers" chapter.

One way I've learned to grow in this area is through the discovery our brain responds to an intellectual threat the same way it does to a physical one. Our amygdala says, "Hey, you're being threatened right now! Get ready to fight or flee!" Because I realize what's going on from a brain chemistry point of view, it helps me respond more rationally. First, I take a deep breath and a pause. This allows me to oxygenate my brain and allow space for a reasonable response instead of being defensive.

You don't have to master this immediately; it takes time. The next time you feel criticized, in the short term, train yourself to say, "Thank you for sharing this feedback with me. I will reflect on what you've shared." You can leave it at that. When you are calm and in control to engage, you can ask questions for clarification and then thank the person for feeling comfortable enough to share his or her feedback with you.

Embrace differences

One of my LinkedIn connections, Jacob, shared with me, "One thing I've learned by working under great leadership is the importance of having diverse thinkers on your team and allowing their freedom of expression."

Melissa "Af" Orroyo-Funderburk, a diversity, equity, and inclusion (DEI) consultant and facilitator agrees and adds, "Metrics and analytics can give us an idea of how well our DEI program is working; hearing our team say they feel included and they truly belong is our actual return on investment. We have to remember there are many verticals to DEI and belonging; as leaders, we must encourage autonomy and empower associates to be decision makers."

My interview with Brenda LaRose in the "Hire: Right People. Right Roles" chapter addresses encouraging diversity, equity, and inclusion.

Here are some additional tips to embrace and prioritize DEI:

- Monitor your thoughts and what you're thinking about.
- Avoid thinking in terms of right and wrong.
- Look for positives in what the person is saying or about the person.
- Stay present and focused instead of retreating into your own head.
- Put yourself in their shoes; how do you want to be treated?

Make work fun

This tip is more natural to pull off for some personalities, but even serious types can cultivate a fun environment. I was speaking to my oldest son, Tristan, as I was working on this book and he told me how much he enjoys his job. He's a senior in college, and he works at a country club in Nashville, Tennessee.

Tristan shared some of the reasons he enjoys his job, and it all boils down to his managers creating a fun place to work. Not all associates will appreciate your attempts to inject fun in the workplace. It's true some people want to go to work, do their jobs, and go home. And that's fine. Create opportunities for associates to have light-hearted fun but don't mandate participation.

Treat mistakes as learning opportunities

Everyone makes mistakes, including you. How do you handle it when your team members make mistakes? Mila, a respondent to a question I posed on LinkedIn, shared, "I want to have a manager who trusts me and allows me to make my own mistakes. This is the only way associates can grow."

The best lessons often come from mistakes, not from textbooks or training. Often, the sting of the misstep is a powerful means for someone to learn what she needs to do better going forward. What can you do, as a manager, to equip your team for success and coach them when they make mistakes?

One idea is to do a lessons learned exercise with your team member using the five questions I introduced in the "Develop: Maximize Potential" chapter. In a supportive environment, start with, "What went well?" This helps your team member see the things she did do well. It's starts on a positive note.

Next, discuss what she could have done differently or better. The goal is for lessons and tangible steps to surface. Allow your associate to lead and share her opinion first. This approach not only allows her to save face, but it's less threatening than if you point out her mistakes. You can add your thoughts after she shares if she hasn't addressed your point of view.

Finally, decide what barriers might have contributed to the mistake so they can be addressed. What needs to change next time (if there is a next time), and how will each of you support the likelihood of success going forward?

Offer praise. And negative feedback.

Steven Young, a research scientist from the Center for Creative Leadership, discovered interesting findings about feedback. Managers who give regular high-quality negative feedback are viewed as more promotable by their own bosses and receive more advancement opportunities.[1] But what do associates think?

Interestingly, a manager's ability to deliver constructive feedback improves coworkers' perceptions of them.[2] Of course, the key word here is *ability*. An ability to deliver negative feedback implies skill. In addition, associates want to receive a higher ratio of positive to negative feedback. Associates who received the most positive feedback were more apt to rate their bosses as highly effective.[3]

You might be wondering, what does high quality for both praise and negative feedback look like? High quality praise should be sincere, specific, and personalized.

Sincere – Everyone can spot fake or forced praise from a mile away, which undermines its effectiveness. If you don't genuinely believe the feedback you're about to give, skip it. Not only will it be devalued, it could damage your influence.

The same holds true for constructive criticism. Sincerity should come through by using a compassionate tone. Kris Macchiarola discussed being direct with respect in the "Emotional Intelligence & Management" section of the "Discover Your Management Style" chapter.

Specific – Generic praise such as, "You did a great job in the meeting!" doesn't offer any indication to your team member what they've done to earn your praise. Remember, behavior that gets rewarded gets repeated. Consider providing behavioral feedback using my C.A.R.E. method.
What was the **C**ontext?
What specific **A**ctions were taken?
What **R**esult did those actions yield?
What are **E**xpectations going forward? (used with constructive feedback)

For example, "Char, yesterday during the team meeting, I was impressed with how you encouraged our quieter team members to share their opinion on the new order tracking system. Your leadership resulted in valuable feedback that might never have surfaced otherwise. Well done."

Being specific is just as important when delivering constructive criticism. The C.A.R.E. method works well for constructive feedback. It's important not to make sweeping generalizations, exaggerations, or assumptions that are a result of interpretation instead of observable facts. For example, here is a poor example of giving feedback:

"Napoleon, it has been brought to my attention you're behaving inappropriately on social media. I'm going to write you up with a formal written warning for your associate file. You'll be required to take a social media policy course next month."

The feedback, "behaving inappropriately," draws a conclusion instead of sharing observable facts. Other interpretations include words such as rude, offensive, and too sensitive.

A better approach is to give specific behavioral feedback without making assumptions, explain the impact or consequences, and offer support for improvement when appropriate.

For example, "Thank you for meeting with me, Napoleon. I've received complaints about two of your comments on LinkedIn, which I've printed for you in these screenshots dated September 6. Both messages violate the company's social media anti-harassment policy. After discussing appropriate action with Human Resources, I've decided not to terminate your employment because I value you as an associate. Instead, I've added a written warning to your associate file. We have a new social media course rolling out, which I will assign for you to take to ensure social media guidelines are clear to avoid a future incident. Is there anything you want to add, or do you have questions?"

In cases where an associate is defensive, it's especially important to rely on facts instead of judgments.

Personalized – Personalized feedback involves tailoring your delivery to the individual. For example, people high in humility are often quite uncomfortable with public praise. Sending an email to the company giving a shout out to your team member could cause irritation or anxiety rather than the warm, fuzzy feeling you were going for.

One idea to personalize feedback is to ask each team member what they consider to be meaningful recognition. I shared examples of personalizing feedback in the "Associate Demotivation: 7 Causes" section under "Feeling undervalued." I found it helpful to create a simple form in Word, and when someone new joined the team, I asked them to share examples of the kinds of recognition they enjoy receiving.

Refer to the section, "Personality & Management" in the "Discover Your Management Style" chapter to find your direct report's personality before giving constructive feedback to tailor your approach based on his or her preferences.

A question I'm often asked is, "How do I start a difficult conversation?" Judy Ringer's *We Have to Talk: A Step-By-Step Checklist for Difficult Conversations* offers useful conversation starters:

I have something I'd like to discuss with you that I think will help us work together more effectively.

I'd like to talk about _____ with you, but first I'd like to get your point of view.

I need your help with what just happened. Do you have a few minutes to talk?

I need your help with something. Can we talk about it (soon)? If the person says, "Sure, let me get back to you," follow up with him.

I think we have different perceptions about _____. I'd like to hear your thinking on this.

I'd like to talk about _____. I think we may have different ideas about how to _____.

I'd like to see if we might reach a better understanding about _____. I really want to hear your feelings about this and share my perspective as well.

Capitalize

As I shared earlier, our tendency is to focus on problems. Underperforming associates take up more time and attention from managers than top performers, who can be left blowing in the wind because they're meeting or exceeding expectations. Our relationship with our top performers should never be placed on autopilot.

It's important to remember the seven causes of demotivation mentioned earlier, specifically, feeling undervalued. Top performers can experience a dampening in their motivation if they perceive their manager takes their effort for granted.

An effective way to help high performers experience sustained motivation is to capitalize on their knowledge, skills, and abilities by discovering where the goals of the individual and the organization intersect. This is where maximum opportunities exist for a true win/win arrangement. Increase the exposure of your top performer by expanding their responsibilities, their network, and their impact—beyond the team if possible.

Discussions in your one-on-one meetings with your associate can help generate great ideas to capitalize on and expand their influence. If your team member values growth, consider sending them to a training class and then creating a special project to benefit the organization while providing a skill-building opportunity on the job.

Increased exposure of your associate should not be a threat to you. People often say a good manager or leader doesn't care who gets the credit. That's true. However, you, as a manager, deserve credit when you show the talents of your team and help the organization benefit from those talents.

You offer your organization so much by expanding the reach of your team members through your development and retention efforts. Don't doubt for a minute people will spot the role you play in elevating the talent of your team. You don't have to be the one "doing" to shine. The mindset you must "do" to get results is the mindset of an individual contributor.

As a manager, you can facilitate, motivate, activate, orchestrate, strategize, ideate, promote, initiate, and many other valuable verbs which don't involve you being the doer. You can be the spark to ignite the greatness in every one of your team members. Doesn't this sound more rewarding than being the best at Excel spreadsheets?

If you're not sure where to start, ask your team! A simple way to find out what your team needs most is by conducting a focus group with them. Ask someone else to facilitate to make sure you get open and honest feedback.

Conducting a Focus Group

If you've never conducted a focus group, here is a sample process you can adapt and use.

1. Draft the invitation to the meeting and share who the facilitator will be. Ask someone apart from human resources to make associates more comfortable.

   Explain the purpose and include the questions to be asked. Distribute at least one week prior to the focus group. Don't mix supervisors with people they supervise.
2. Serve refreshments – simple is fine (coffee and tea in the morning, drinks and pretzels or cookies in the afternoon).
3. Let the facilitator make their own introduction.

Explain why everyone is there ("Your manager, Lacey, wants to [state objective of the focus group] and has asked me to help by getting your thoughts."). The facilitator should post his or her name and email on a sheet of flip chart paper. This is the time to clarify the process for confidentiality. For example:

a) Participants can contact the facilitator after the focus group session if they have questions or additional information they want to share.
b) Participants can leave behind the booklets they'll be using if they want to write down something they'd rather not share in front of the group. Instruct them to draw a box around any items on their list they didn't have the comfort to share with the group.
c) The facilitator will stay in the room for 15 minutes after the focus group ends if anyone wants to remain behind to speak with him or her.

Emphasize the information given is confidential and will not be attributed to individuals. Let participants know they will receive a summary of the information once the process has concluded. Repeat the purpose and have the questions you will be asking at the top of each page of flip chart paper. Ask if participants have any questions before you begin.

4. Use a nominal group technique.

Give each person a blank sheet of 8 ½ x 11 paper and ask them to fold it in half to create an 8 ½ x 5 ½ booklet. Mark the cover as number 1, the inside sheets 2 and 3 and the back cover 4. They will use this to list their responses to each of the four questions.

5. Begin with question 1: "What's working? What successes are you having?"

Ask them to jot down their responses to this question on the cover of the booklet they made. Give them two-to-three minutes to do this and wait until everyone is finished. Use a round-robin format to go around the group so each person can give one response to the question.

Write down everything they say, point by point, on flip chart paper so they can see exactly what information you're gathering. If you need to summarize a response, check with the person to be sure they agree with the summary you write. Go around the group twice. When you have finished the second round, ask if there are any other items people want to add from their lists.

6. When you have captured all their information, return to the beginning of the list and check for agreement. Ask how many people (by show of hands) agree with each of the statements presented, going through the statements one at a time. Write the number in parentheses next to the response (using a different color marker). This allows you to rank order the responses to gauge consensus within the group.

7. Repeat the above process with the remaining three questions:
    a) What would you prefer to see done better, differently?
    b) What's preventing these improvements? (barriers)
    c) How could you help?

8. At the conclusion of the focus group, remind people they can leave their sheet with you and you will remain in the room for 15 minutes after the focus group session if anyone wants to speak with you privately.

9. When you transcribe comments from the focus group, list responses according to frequency under each question. Start with most frequent responses and work down, such as the top ten. Summarize them into themes and use quotes from the focus group to offer detail and richness.

10. Final thoughts
    - Fewer, broad questions work better than a laundry list of specific questions.
    - Recording is not recommended, especially if you want candor, because it makes people nervous.
    - The described method adapts SWOT (strengths, weaknesses, opportunities, and threats) analysis as the foundation of your focus group:
        a) What's working? What success is your team having?
        b) What needs to be done better, differently, more?
        c) What's preventing these improvements?
        d) What might you do that could help?

The data gathered from your team's feedback will help you decide what retention strategies will be most meaningful to them. It's important to act on feedback you receive and keep them in the loop with status check-ins in team meetings. Asking for feedback and not doing anything with it is worse than not asking for feedback at all.

My hope is this chapter gave you a few solid strategies to increase associate retention on your team. The focus group will certainly yield ideas for action! Now, let's move on to discuss one of the least favorite manager responsibilities, associate terminations.

CHAPTER 11

OFFBOARD: DISCHARGE WITH DIGNITY

"Firing is not something you do to someone: firing is something you do for someone."

Larry Winget, author, speaker

In 10 years of managing people, I've terminated employment of only one person. Associates I've personally hired performed as expected. The few associates I've had with performance concerns were on the team when I joined. In most cases, I helped them turn their performance around.

Three associates I managed should have been released, but I was unable to separate them from the organization because of company politics. One associate was hired by the company president and was the sixth associate in a 5,000-person company, and two associates were members of a protected class, which influenced HR's decision not to allow termination for fear of a lawsuit despite major, documented performance concerns.

Because I've not personally released many associates, I conducted interviews and a survey of managers who've released associates to share their experiences. One thing is certain—no one I've encountered while writing this book enjoys releasing people.

I've worked with a lot of clients who've been fired. In most cases, the company did the person a favor in the long run. They weren't happy in their job but weren't able to walk away, usually because of the security of their paycheck.

Regardless of a termination being a hidden blessing, it's important to let an associate go in a way that retains their dignity. Most people come to work wanting to do a good job. And some people just can't rise to the requirements of the role. There's no need to crush their spirit in the process.

I've had dozens of conversations with clients who were fired from their employment and, while there are two sides to every story, I've noticed disturbing trends with the stories I've heard. In several cases, the lack of respect shown to the associate was alarming.

Amy, a manager herself, had been a top performer in her organization for well over a decade. She was a natural at developing talent in her associates, and her investment in them resulted in many of her direct reports receiving promotions.

Amy was looking for a new challenge in the organization and decided to take on a new role. Amy is a goal-oriented, strategic thinker. She's innovative and loves challenging her team to grow their capabilities. In her new role, Amy found herself reporting to a manager who didn't appreciate her strengths. Her new manager, Julie, had a finance background and was a detail-oriented micro-manager.

Amy's efforts to work successfully with Julie proved fruitless. Julie made up her mind she wanted Amy off the team. She began writing Amy up for everything she could think of. Instead of giving Amy constructive feedback, she criticized her, including telling another manager, "Amy drives me crazy" in Amy's presence.

Julie began assigning projects with aggressive and unreasonable deadlines so Amy couldn't possibly submit her deliverables by the deadline, enabling Julie to write her up and collect enough manufactured offenses to terminate her.

Amy's story is too common. A manager and a direct report have opposing personalities and work styles, and rather than embracing differences and trying to work more effectively together, the manager becomes either overtly aggressive or passive aggressive, which creates a tense environment. Some managers go so far as to make the workplace environment hostile enough for the associate to quit. And if the associate doesn't quit, the manager begins to take action to terminate the associate.

Two of the most detrimental outcomes of this management behavior are damage to the confidence of the associate and lowered team morale. Oftentimes, when this happens, the associate internalizes the situation as a personal failure. If a person isn't a fit for a role, there's no reason we should make them believe they're a failure.

I've heard from managers who have had plenty of compassion for associates they have released. Some associates truly needed to be released, and it was an unpleasant situation for everyone involved.

Brian Ray, former Vice President of Support Services at Chick-fil-A, shared the following thoughts with me regarding off-boarding:

Offboarding starts with onboarding. If you don't start the onboarding process well, you're marching toward offboarding. One of the things that [is] so incredibly important [is] expectations. And expectations might change. If you don't touch it once a week, it's going to be a problem. It's the continued adjustment of expectations, feedback, and work to be accomplished.

If somebody comes in the door, and you realize they're good at X, and even better at Y, and if I can get them into Z, everybody is going to love that. So that's part of the conversation going in the door.

"This is what we've hired you for, and we're excited about that, and we will continue to look for opportunities to maximize your contribution and your growth." Those are two key words, by the way. As far as the associate is concerned and the manager making the most of that, it's contribution. Everybody wants to feel like they're contributing. And they want to grow—and not just financially. That's the setting for the onboarding, training, development, and retaining.

But then you realize they're unhappy, or something else is going on, and you must release them. And so the phrase that's really important is that if you do anything other than "speak the truth in love" you are headed for disaster. Most people think speaking the truth in love is either/or. They think love is not telling them the truth. That's not love; that's a lie. So, that's a really important factor.

Let's say you've got someone that not only needs to leave the position, they have to leave the company. You must have two of you doing it. Don't do it alone. The usual partnership is the supervisor and an HR rep. They've put them on a performance plan, and they get three times before you release them. You have to have a plan, you have to stay with the plan, and you have to have a partner.

I can remember a situation with a maintenance staffer. There was me, the HR director and the individual. By the time it got to me, there had already been conversations. I had already been in on two conversations, and we had done a really good job of explaining, "If you do X or you don't do Y, we're going to have to release you."

I remember this very clearly. We were in the "you've got to go" conversation. There were three of us and him. It was the same team in the meeting. And I was the one to say, "I'm so sorry, were going to have to let you go." And the guy lunged for me, physically, ready to attack me. And they caught him and had to usher him out, and it was really awful. He was saying something along the lines of, "You never told me!" So you can do everything well, but it still turns out poorly.

Brian advised to make every positive effort to put it in writing for them to understand what it is they are, or are not, doing that needs to change for the sake of clarity to make sure everyone is on the same page. Include the highlights from the conversation about "what happened" and "what's going to happen."

As mentioned, I conducted surveys of people with experience releasing associates. I wanted to know what they thought went well, what didn't go well, and what they would change with the benefit of hindsight.

Paul, who works in human resources, shared a story about a team member who had been with the organization for more than 20 years and was having a difficult time adjusting to new processes.

Paul explained, "She received a lot of training and understood the principles, but she had a difficult time changing her attitude to the new way of doing things. Her work demeanor continued to deteriorate and was affecting the entire team. Her leaders sat down and discussed it with her to determine what could change to help her with the transition. She agreed to a few changes but, within three weeks, she was back to the bad ways. We ended up terminating her. She did not seem to understand why, but the team's productivity and attitude increased substantially after she left."

Hindsight is 20/20, and I asked Paul what he learned from the experience. He indicated what went well was the dramatic change in the team. In addition, they spent time with the associate, fully documenting and sharing expectations in the first counseling meeting.

What could have been better? "We still review to see what we might have been able to do to help her better understand the situation. She did not understand why she was being let go, and that bothers us, but we could not afford more time to work on it."

In the end, Paul suggested the only thing he might change was getting her an independent coach who might help her better understand how her actions were affecting the team.

Information Technology manager, Steve, shared the time he hired a recent college graduate.

"He was sharp and showed a lot of potential. Unfortunately, he spent a lot of time at work on social media and surfing the internet, and his completion numbers for tasks were the lowest on the team. Team members tried to coach him to change his behavior, and as the manager I had a conversation with him regarding expectations for the job. He continued spending too much time on nonwork tasks. Since he was within the first 90 days, I let him go and gave him feedback on why I was letting him go. Several years later he contacted me and thanked me for the training he had received during that short period, because he went on to use the training for a successful career."

When I asked Steve what went well and what he would change, he said he probably wouldn't change anything and added, "You always hope the person fired learns from the situation, and in this case, he appears to have done so."

Steve shared in a few cases he was able to encourage the person to leave on their own, and they found a new job. In all cases, he emphasized the importance of HR having a clear process to follow, which helped him give associates the information they needed. Most of Steve's terminations occurred within the first 90 days.

He shared in another case, he later heard the person committed suicide because he had trouble holding down a job. He finds tenured associates the most challenging to let go because of rigid processes and policies. Most companies require a documented verbal warning, a write up for continued issues with action plan, a second write up with action plan, and a third write up to be fired.

If the associate showed improvement within six months, the first write up no longer applied, and if the associate returned to the bad behaviors, the process started all over again. Steve added, "This tedious process often discourages managers from removing poor performers, and they just accept them on team."

Sometimes, firing an associate isn't absolutely necessary. Michael, another manager who responded to my survey for this book, shared, "Once, I had to terminate someone who deserved it. We had the smoking gun, but for the benefit of the culture, we looked past it and rehabilitated him."

Other times, leadership could have avoided the resulting termination.

Maya shares:

I was assigned the task of terminating an underachieving salesperson. No one wanted to do it, and they figured if I was leading people, I needed experience. "So here goes," I thought to myself. My manager said, "It's simple. He hasn't reached the 90-day probationary period anyway, and in Florida you don't need to give a reason to fire. We just need to be professional and terminate in a formal manner."

Now what kind of concrete information do we have on this guy?! He was late a few times, [and] we said something, but we never formally sat him down about it to warn why he shouldn't be late again. No verbal, first, or second write up. The fact was he could not sell. With more experience now, I realize that we set him up for failure by not setting up-front expectations. We trained with a shadowing technique, but if you didn't catch on, you were out. If we were committed to a process of setting the expectations for the role, training on the systems and processes to be successful in the role, we may not have had to terminate this person.

Maya's right.

Thoughtful preparation and execution of the steps discussed in chapters five, seven, eight, nine, and ten (hiring, onboarding, training, developing, and retaining) sets everyone up for success.

June experienced the negative impact of this firsthand. She shared a recent termination story:

Alexander had been promoted over the course of nine years, more out of obligation and doing his current job rather than due to merit and knowledge, by several previous managers.

By the time Alexander was transitioned to my team, he did not possess the skills of a senior business intelligence analyst. My perception was that no one had the heart, nor wherewithal, to work on building him up. I first had the toughest conversation of my life.

"Alexander, your skills have not developed to the level of a senior intelligence analyst. I'd like to work with you on a plan to get you there." What I was not prepared for was his response. "I've never been told that before," he replied.

The plan consisted of projects for him to develop his skills and test his knowledge. I spent hours coaching on methods, formulas, strategies, and formatting regularly, several days a week. With each week, he missed key milestones, and I had to remind him that he was not performing. After six months of soul crushing (his and mine) conversations, I began to work with HR on messaging his termination.

The day finally came.

"Alexander, you have missed several key milestones, failed to implement the skills and knowledge we've worked on together. As of today, we will no longer continue your employment. I have Jessica from HR here to help you through this transition today. Thank you for your efforts." Again, his response surprised me, "I had no idea that I was not meeting expectations."

June's final thoughts on Alexander's termination are sentiments shared by others who completed the survey. "The amount of documentation managers are expected to prepare is insurmountable and takes way too much time. The weekly meetings of him not meeting performance drained me. I was resentful of everyone who had managed him previously, and I was angry. What a disservice they did to him! He may have been employed, but he got nothing out of it he could take to a new job. I left the company a few months later," she said.

Not only do excessively burdensome processes discourage managers from releasing associates when it's truly necessary, they demotivate and discourage managers, which can create further associate disengagement across the management team. It demotivates the other team members to see an associate with poor performance "get away with it."

Here are suggestions to lessen the burden of performance documentation:

1. **Reduce duplication of effort** – After having a performance conversation with an associate, send a follow up email to the individual with the information required for formal documentation as much as possible. This will allow you to document the conversation and complete formal documentation by pasting from the email, saving duplication of effort.

2. **Automate where possible** – Use audio software or recording apps to log occurrences for later transcription for documentation.

3. **Manage your time** – Break your documentation into smaller chunks. Instead of tackling in a two-hour time block, spend two thirty-minute chunks over two days. If you're afraid you'll forget details, record a voice memo for yourself on a mobile phone app similar to Rev Recorder. This keeps the activity from planting itself firmly in your burnout zone.

4. **Increase documentation quality** – Build a stronger case in less time. Human Resources doesn't always understand the implications or context of what you're documenting. Make it easier for them to support you. For example, instead of saying, "The associate cleared 50 task list items and entered no notes," connect the dots on the business implications. For example, "50 cleared task list items without automated notes confirms tasks were not performed by the associate, which

indicates an attempt to receive credit for work that was not performed." See the difference? Include the context and business impact in all documentation.

I've worked in companies that took a silent stance whenever someone was let go. This is not a good idea. It creates confusion for people collaborating with the associate when their emails aren't answered or are returned undelivered. When you don't proactively communicate an associate's termination, the gossip mill will surely manage the communication on your behalf. This erodes people's confidence in leadership and has a negative impact on the company culture. When announcing an associate termination, be brief, avoid drama, and stick to the facts:

"Vance Pants no longer works at STB. Our transition plan is for Doug Thompson to be the interim lead for Vance's projects. If you have any questions, please contact Kristin Olson-Kott."

During my interview with Brenda LaRose, she shared she's known leaders who offboard very well. Their approach with the associate is, "This is not a great fit. How can we help? How can we help you find another position?" The candidate leaves the organization believing good intent from their manager, and even though they've been fired, the individual still admires and respects the person who fired them.

Brenda adds, "You want the people who worked for you to say, 'I would do anything to work for that leader. They're a great leader.' Everyone else on the team sees how you dealt with the person you offboarded, and it's important to have a good reputation as a leader."

Ultimately, if you hire the right people, onboard them well, train them effectively, and develop them to their potential, you should find yourself in termination situations a lot less. It's important to get the right people into the right roles, because, as you now know, you can't train or develop a wrong fit into a right one.

In the final chapter, I want to shift from focusing on your associates to focusing on you. As you progress through your career journey, you should be aware of the behaviors associated with career success and those leading to a career flaming out. In "Career Derailers," I'll share the research on career stallers and career flow.

CHAPTER 12

CAREER DERAILERS

> "Just imagine how much you'd get done if you stopped actively sabotaging your own work."
>
> *Seth Godin, author*

I believe people sabotage themselves without realizing it. While this book largely covers what makes an effective manager, it's important to address the behaviors that get in the way of promotion and success.

Korn Ferry, a global organizational consulting firm, has done extensive research on the behavioral traits that halt a person's career in its tracks, known as **career derailers**. They've also researched the behavioral traits correlated to career flow and further promotion.[1] What I find useful about their research is they've broken down the traits correlated to promotion on three levels:

- Individual contributors
- Managers
- Executives

Career Derailers

The following eight traits are correlated with stalling a person's career at all levels (individual, manager, and executive). These are the behaviors Korn

Ferry found most likely to deter career growth and stop forward movement in one's career path:

1. **Unable to adapt to differences** – Has trouble working with or adapting to new bosses, strategies, plans, or programs

2. **Overly ambitious** – Excessively focused on self and upward career movement, sometimes at the expense of others

3. **Arrogance** – Always thinks he/she has the right answers, dismisses input of others, can be cold, makes others feel inferior, keeps distance between him/herself and others

4. **Betrays trust** – Says one thing and means or does another, is unpredictable or inconsistent, fails to follow through on commitments

5. **Lack of composure** – Handles stress poorly, gets emotional when things don't go as planned, hostile or sarcastic, makes poor or snap decisions under pressure, performance tanks when things get tough

6. **Defensiveness** – Not open to criticism, denies mistakes and faults, kills the messenger, blames others, doesn't listen to negative feedback, doesn't share personal limitations with others

7. **Insensitive to others** – Intimidating style, makes others feel bad, doesn't care or think about how he/she affects others, doesn't follow interpersonal cues, doesn't care or ask about others' needs

8. **Overmanaging** – Meddles, doesn't empower others, doesn't develop direct reports well, poor delegator, doesn't get the most out of people

   Something to note about overmanaging is there are three personality characteristics that contribute to micro-managing behavior: low trust, high perfectionism, and detail-orientation.

Have you ever received feedback on any of these traits? If so, I recommend adding the behaviors you struggle with to your development plan as a priority. For help soliciting feedback, refer to the five questions in "Develop: Maximize Potential" and conducting a focus group as detailed in "Retain: Value Your Treasure" chapter.

No one is perfect, and we're all a work in progress. But if these behaviors are left unchecked they will most certainly lead to a career flame out in a matter of time.

When I was working in information technology, an IT leader had climbed the ladder quickly from an individual contributor to the executive level. He had a reputation of being arrogant and once said to a direct report, "I pay you to do, not to think" after the associate offered an opinion.

Given his meteoric rise, it's tempting to believe the saying, "Nice guys finish last" is true. Bad behavior eventually catches up to a person when enough people have the courage to report it. People who exhibit these behaviors consistently become a liability to an organization. Eventually, this executive was fired from the company.

On the flip side of the career derailer coin is **career flow**. Korn Ferry's research found the following traits are correlated to receiving a promotion.[2]

Promotional Competencies for Individual Contributors

1. **Action-Orientation** – Enjoys working hard, is full of energy, not fearful of acting, and seizes more opportunities than others
2. **Perseverance** – Pursues everything with energy, drive, and a need to finish; seldom gives up in the face of resistance or setbacks

Promotional Competencies for Managers

1. **Action-Orientation** – Enjoys working hard, is full of energy, is not fearful of acting, and seizes more opportunities than others
2. **Boss Relationships** – Relates and responds well to bosses, coachable, willing to work hard for a good boss, open to learning from others who've been there before
3. **Customer Focus** – Dedicated to meeting expectations and requirements of internal and external customers, acts with customers in mind, gets first-hand customer information for improvements in products and services, establishes and maintains trust, and builds effective customer relationships
4. **Decision Quality** – Makes good decisions, most solutions turn out to be correct, sought out by others for advice
5. **Informing Others** – Provides information people need to know to do their jobs and so people can make accurate decisions, is timely with information

6. **Intellectual Horsepower** – Is bright and intelligent, deals with concepts and complexity comfortably, described as intellectually sharp, capable, and agile

7. **Learning on the Fly** – Learns quickly when facing new problems, open to change, relentless, versatile learner, analyzes success and failure for improvement, experiments, will try anything to find solutions, enjoys the challenge of unfamiliar tasks, and quickly grasps the essence and underlying structure of anything

8. **Peer Relationships** – Can quickly find common ground, represents own interests yet is fair to others, easily gains trust and support of peers, encourages collaboration, candid with peers, and is seen as cooperative

9. **Drive for Results** – Can be counted on to exceed goals, consistently one of the top performers, bottom-line oriented, steadfastly pushes self and others for results

10. **Time Management** – Uses time effectively and efficiently, values time, concentrates efforts on important priorities, gets more done in less time than others, can attend to a broader range of activities

Promotional Competencies for Executives

The following traits are correlated with promotion at the executive level. The traits with asterisks (*) are specific to promotion of executives. The traits without asterisks are shared traits with managers for promotion.

1. **Boss Relationships** – Relates and responds well to bosses, coachable, willing to work hard for a good boss, open to learning from others who've been there before

2. ***Comfort with Higher Management** – Can deal comfortably with more senior managers, understands how senior managers think, can present to more senior managers without undue tension or nervousness

3. **Customer Focus** – Dedicated to meeting expectations and requirements of internal and external customers, acts with customers in mind, gets first-hand customer information for improvements in

products and services, establishes and maintains trust, and builds effective customer relationships

4. ***Functional/Technical Skills** – Has the functional and technical knowledge and skills to do the job at a high level of accomplishment

5. **Learning on the Fly** – Learns quickly when facing new problems, open to change, relentless, versatile learner, analyzes success and failure for improvement, experiments, will try anything to find solutions, enjoys the challenge of unfamiliar tasks, quickly grasps the essence and underlying structure of anything

6. ***Listening** – Practices attentive and active listening, has patience to hear people out, can accurately restate opinions of others even when he/she disagrees

7. **Peer Relationships** – Can quickly find common ground, represents own interests yet is fair to others, easily gains trust and support of peers, encourages collaboration, candid with peers, and is seen as cooperative

8. ***Planning** – Accurately scopes length and difficulty of projects, sets objectives and goals, breaks down work into process steps, develops schedules, anticipates problems, measures performance against goals, and evaluates results

9. **Drive for Results** – Can be counted on to exceed goals, consistently one of the top performers, bottom-line oriented, steadfastly pushes self and others for results

10. ***Total Work Systems** – Dedicated to providing organization-wide common systems, seeks to reduce variance in organizational processes, committed to continuous improvement through empowerment and management by data, leverages technology to positively impact quality, creates a learning environment, willing to re-engineer processes from scratch, delivers the highest quality products and services, which meet customer needs

If you are interested in a vertical career path that includes promotional opportunities, I recommend adding some of these traits to your formal development plan. If you don't have a formal development plan, you can follow the steps in the "Develop: Maximize Potential" chapter to create one.

Obtain feedback from your manager to prioritize the traits for development. To learn more about career stallers and stoppers, including roadmaps to remediate and develop career staller and career flow behaviors, respectively, I recommend getting a copy of the book, *FYI For Your Improvement* by Michael M. Lombardo and Robert W. Eichinger.

It is my hope you have more tools available to you in your management toolkit to hire, onboard, train, develop, retain, and offboard your associates, while continuously working on your own personal and professional development, striving to avoid career derailers.

The fact you read this book tells me you are committed to a growth mindset. Perfection is impossible but armed with the tools and tips in this book, you have what you need to be the kind of manager who earns respect and gets results.

FINAL THOUGHTS

On average, you could spend **40 years** of your life working.

If you take four weeks off, annually, you'll spend **76,800 hours** at work, equaling **9,600 days** of your life.

With an average life span of **28,000 days**, that represents a **full third** of your days on Earth spent **working**.

Please don't make those days unhappy for yourself.

Or anyone else.

Kristin

AFTERWORD

I've heard many stories of managers who didn't measure up. I decided to celebrate the difference a capable manager can make by highlighting two great managers, one in the foreword and one in afterword.

In the foreword, Evans describes how his future manager, Henry, saw his potential and believed in him. Here, Nancy shares a tribute to her former manager, Petrina. I hope this encourages you to pursue continuous management skill development. You have the chance to leave a legacy!

Enjoy Nancy's tribute:

Seldom do we take the time to look back and genuinely value those managers who have made a difference in the people they manage. These are my observations from when I had the good fortune to work for a great manager.

Greatness comes in many forms. No single skill set, knowledge base, or personality traits can define a great manager. Instead, greatness comes from a fusion of qualities, emotional intelligence, and talents. Petrina DeKoster is the type of leader that encompasses greatness.

Upon reflecting on my time working for Petrina, her best attributes can be defined as GREAT.

G = Genuine – No pretentiousness here; Petrina is the real deal. She truly cared deeply about her team members and shared stories of her successes and failures.

R = Respectful – Petrina was always professional in conversations, instructions, and coaching. She understood people have lives outside of work and was mindful of late-breaking requests.

E = Engaging – Petrina could rally the troops, create passion for excellence, and reward based on an individual's goals.

A = Advocate – Career growth requires a strong promoter; Petrina was that manager. She broadly shared her associates' successes with senior leaders and endorsed associates for advancement.

T = Team – Petrina had the superpowers to quickly drive a team from forming – storming – norming to performing. She knew what it took to build a high-performing team and provided the required support so that the team had the tools needed to succeed.

Thank you for the opportunity to describe a great manager.

Nancy Kazmierski
Charlotte, North Carolina, September 2019

REFERENCES

Introduction

1. Amy Adkins, "Only One in 10 People Possess the Talent to Manage," Gallup, Gallup, Inc., April 13, 2015, https://www.gallup.com/workplace/236579/one-people-possess-talent-manage.aspx.

Chapter 1

1. Gallup *State of the Global Workplace*, Gallup Press, 2017.
2. J. Sterling Livingston, "The Myth of the Well-Educated Manager," *Harvard Business Review*, 1971, https://hbr.org/1971/01/myth-of-the-well-educated-manager).

Chapter 2

1. Jim Harter, "Managers Account for 70% Variance in Employee Engagement," Gallup, Inc., 2015, https://news.gallup.com/businessjournal/182792/managers-account-variance-employee-engagement.aspx.
2. Ibid.

Chapter 3

1. WhatIs, Tech Target, 2019, https://whatis.techtarget.com/definition/gig-economy.
2. Amy Adkins, "Only One in 10 People Possess the Talent to Manage," Gallup, Inc., 2015, https://www.gallup.com/workplace/236579/one-people-possess-talent-manage.aspx.
3. ReWork, Google, https://rework.withgoogle.com/.
4. "Guide: Care Professionally and Personally for Your Team," Re:Work, Google, Retrieved September 27, 2019, from https://rework.withgoogle.com/guides/managers-care-professionally-personally-for-team/steps/introduction/.
5. Christina Boedker, Richard Vidgen, Kieron Meagher, Julie Cogin, Jan Mouritsen, Jonathon Mark Runnalls, *Leadership, Culture and Management Practices of High Performing Workplaces in Australia: The High Performing Workplaces Index*, HPW, Society for Knowledge Economics, 2011,

http://www.hpw.org.au/uploads/5/9/1/7/59177601/boedker_vidgen_meagher_cogin_mou ritsen_and_runnalls_2011_high_performing_workplaces_index_october_6_2011.pdf.

Chapter 4

1. Travis Bradberry, "7 Ways Managers Motivate and Demotivate People," The Ladders, 2018, https://www.theladders.com/career-advice/7-ways-managers-motivate-and-demotivate-employeees.

2. Michael Page, "7 Causes of Employee Demotivation", Michael Page, Retrieved September 28, 2019 from https://www.michaelpage.co.uk/advice/management-advice/development-and-retention/seven-reasons-employee-demotivation.

3. Sturt, Todd Nordstrom, Kevin Ames and Gary Beckstrand, *Appreciation: Celebrating People, Inspiring* Greatness, O.C. Tanner Institute, 2017.

Chapter 5

1. Mark Murphy, "Why New Hires Fail (Emotional Intelligence Vs. Skills)", Leadership IQ, Retrieved September 28, 2019 from https://www.leadershipiq.com/blogs/leadershipiq/35354241-why-new-hires-fail-emotional-intelligence-vs-skills.

Chapter 6

1. Peter Flade, Jim Asplund, Gwen Elliot, "Employees Who Use Their Strengths Outperform Those Who Don't" 2015, Gallup, Inc., 2015, https://www.gallup.com/workplace/236561/employees-strengths-outperform-don.aspx

Chapter 8

1. Ken Phillips, "How Much is Scrap Learning Costing Your Organization?", Association for Talent Development, 2016, https://www.td.org/insights/how-much-is-scrap-learning-costing-your-organization.

2. Michael Beer, Magnus Finnström, Derek Schrader, "Why Leadership Training Fails – and What to Do About It," *Harvard Business Review,* 2016, https://hbr.org/2016/10/why-leadership-training-fails-and-what-to-do-about-it.

Chapter 10

1. Stephen Young, "The Truth About Negative Feedback," Talent Economy, 2017, https://www.chieflearningofficer.com/2017/10/12/negative-feedback.

2. Ibid.

3. Ibid.

4.   Dawn Metcalfe, *The HardTalk™ Handbook*, CreateSpace Independent Publishing Platform, 2018.

Chapter 12

1.   Lombardo, Michael M., and Robert W. Eichinger, *FYI: For Your Improvement: A Guide for Development and Coaching 4th edition*, Lominger Ltd Inc, 2004.

2.   Ibid.

APPENDIX

The 7 Causes of Associate Demotivation

Lack of flexibility

Short-term objectives with no career vision

Feeling undervalued

No development opportunities

Poor leadership

Conflict

Unrealistic workload

Sample Onboarding Process

1. Decide onboarding **length** and **activities**, such as a three-to- four-week plan
2. Outline **key focus areas** for associate's first 60-90 days
3. Provide a **week-by-week** on-boarding overview

Create a basic outline for each week, including key individuals for relationship building related to the focus areas you outlined above. This could include team members, project team members, internal and external stakeholders, clients, customers, peers, and strategic partners. An onboarding outline might include:

- On-boarding task
- Purpose
- Meetings to schedule
- Responsible party
- Notes or info to review in advance of meeting

Set priorities for the first 60-90 days. For example:

- Establish leadership of team (coaching, development, work status)
- Ensure transition strategy (if applicable)
- Assess current state of key projects
- Include brief bullets of a "Beyond 90 Days" plan (Priorities can be set later.)

Development Planning Best Practices

The following list contains 10 best practices you can share with associates to help them increase the success of their development plans.

Be selective – Decide critical skills that you need to develop based on stated career goals. Set reasonable goals you can accomplish in a realistic timeframe.

Ask for detailed feedback – Seek behavioral feedback on your development needs from others you work with. Ask questions to get specific examples. When? Where? With whom? In what settings? Under what conditions? How often?

Identify what you need to start, stop, and continue doing.

Learn from mentors – Find several mentors who excel in one area you want to grow instead of trying to find one person who has everything. Reduce what they do (and don't do) to a set of practices to incorporate into your behavior.

Read at least two books covering your needed area of development – What are how-to*s* of the skill? How is the skill best learned?

Read biographies – Learn from people who possess the skill you want to build.

Learn from a course – Choose a course that offers a chance to practice the skill.

Take on a stretch task – Seventy percent of skill development occurs on the job. Track the positive and negative aspects of your skill performance and note everything you want to do differently or better next time.

Track improvements – Set goals for yourself and celebrate as you reach milestones. For example, if you're working on approachability, set a goal to initiate a conversation with five new people weekly.

Get regular feedback – Ask both people who know you well and those who haven't known you long, to gain different points of view.

The 5 Questions

What's working?

This question is designed to surface the benefits and positives of your associate's development progress. How can you leverage or expand on her progress?

What needs to be done better or differently?

This question introduces the need for change in a nonthreatening way that opens people to possibilities. It is future-focused. By looking across the suggestions, begin to think about what the changes have in common so that they can be grouped, then focus on the critical few.

What's preventing improvement?

This question is designed to surface barriers to the changes. Again, look at what the barriers have in common, focusing on the critical few. This is a good time to ask about possible obstacles that might impede progress on the things that need to be done better or differently.

If you could make one change, what would it be?

This question can bring a strong focus on the most important change that needs to be made. Is this the best place to start?

How can I help?

1. Asking people how they might help themselves accomplishes two things: She might recognize that she is the barrier to improvement, and something about her behavior or attitude needs to change.

2. You can develop a resource inventory based on skills, talent, knowledge, experience, etc., in the group to best assign staff projects.

Development Planning Worksheet

Current Role/Next Role	Key Required Strengths/Skills	Mentor Recommended Experiences/Resources
Current Role - Summary of responsibilities/oversight	Based on current expectations and defined responsibilities	e.g. Side-by-sides, mentor, skill-based mentoring, on-the-job stretch tasks
Next Role - Summary of responsibilities/oversight	Based on research/discussion with someone in relevant role	e.g. Side-by-sides, mentor, skill-based mentoring, on-the-job stretch tasks

Action Plan

COMPETENCY	BEFORE STATE	CAUSES	AFTER STATE	DEVELOPMENT TASK	NEXT STEPS
Enter each competency to develop in this column	How would you describe yourself as it relates to this skill, currently?	What causes might explain your current skill level in this competency? For example, if you're not skilled in delegating, is it because you aren't familiar with delegation best practices or do you have difficulty letting go of tasks?	What would you like this competency to look like in you **after** you've increased your effectiveness in this skill?	What are some development tasks that will lead to the desired after state?	List any actions to take.
Delegate	I have trouble delegating. I worry the task won't be done right.	I struggle with perfectionism and I can be critical of other people's lack of attention to detail.	I'd like to be able to let go of my unrealistic standards and trust others to take on some of the tasks that have become routine for me.	I plan to discuss my perfectionism with my mentor for advice and then identify a task and delegate to a team member whom I trust and who is well-suited for the task.	Schedule meeting with my mentor for next week to discuss.

Career Derailers

The following eight traits are correlated with stalling a person's career at all levels (individual, manager, and executive). These behaviors are most likely to deter career growth and stop forward movement:

Unable to adapt to differences – Has trouble working with or adapting to new bosses, strategies, plans, or programs

Overly ambitious – Excessively focused on self and upward career movement, sometimes at the expense of others

Arrogance – Always thinks he/she has the right answers, dismisses input of others, can be cold, makes others feel inferior, keeps distance between him/herself and others

Betrays trust – Says one thing and means or does another, is unpredictable or inconsistent, fails to follow through on commitments

Lack of composure – Handles stress poorly, gets emotional when things don't go as planned, hostile or sarcastic, makes poor or snap decisions under pressure, performance tanks when things get tough

Defensiveness – Not open to criticism, denies mistakes and faults, kills the messenger, blames others, doesn't listen to negative feedback, doesn't share personal limitations with others

Insensitive to others – Intimidating style, makes others feel bad, doesn't care or think about how he/she affects others, doesn't follow interpersonal cues, doesn't care or ask about other's needs

Overmanaging – Meddles, doesn't empower others, doesn't develop direct reports well, poor delegator, doesn't get the most out of people

Sample YouMap®

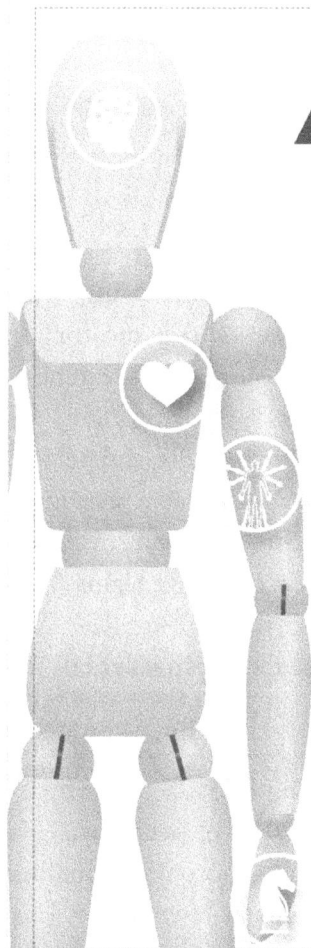

PERSONALIZED YOUMAP® FOR:

ELLIE FOWLER

How I'm Wired

Systematic thinker, accurate, cautious, deeply engaged with whatever they do, quick with calculations, precise, uncompromising

What I Value

Inner Harmony, Trust, Wisdom, Compassion, Love/Connection, Making a difference, Generosity, Pleasure

My Strengths

Harmony, Input, Includer, Restorative, Analytical

Skills I Enjoy

Budget, Envision, Ideate, Innovate, Strategize, Collaborate, Use Intuition, Mentor, Motivate, Analyze, Observe, Research, Study, Delegate, Computer Skills, Numeric Accuracy

My Unique Contribution

Trust and consensus-builder who accepts and values others. A curious, resourceful and systematic thinker; enjoys analyzing and digging into problems to find reasons and causes to solve problems collaboratively and strategize solutions as part of a team.

© 2015 YouMap LLC • All Rights Reserved
www.MyYouMap.com

YouMap® is a registered trademark of YouMap LLC.
Unauthorized use or reproduction of the YouMap® Career Profile is strictly prohibited.

ABOUT THE AUTHOR

KRISTIN SHERRY is a career consultant, author, speaker, and managing partner of YouMap, LLC. She is the creator of the YouMap® profile, a holistic self-awareness tool that uncovers client, associate, and student strengths, values, preferred skills, and personality-based interests. A former learning and development leader at a Fortune 20 company, Kristin managed the company's learning strategy and coached leaders and their teams.

Her previous book, *YouMap: Find Yourself. Blaze Your Path. Show the World!* launched November 8, 2018, and reached #1 best-seller on Amazon in five countries, including the United States.

Her career discovery and empowerment book, *Follow Your Star: Career Lessons I Learned from Mom,* and her interviewing book, *5 Surprising Steps to Land the Job NOW!,* were released in 2016 and 2017, respectively.

Kristin was a DisruptHR speaker, interviewed on Wharton Business Radio's "Career Talk," featured on Inc.com and in *Entrepreneur Magazine,* and was an invited author and speaker at the Emirates Literature Festival, the world's largest international book festival. She is also a member of The Authors Guild.

Kristin serves on the Board of Directors of Crossroads Career®, a faith-based 501(c)3 nonprofit organization that helps the unfulfilled, misemployed, and unemployed to hear God calling, get the right job, and maximize their career. She lives in North Carolina with her husband Xander and their children.

Work with the Author

SPEAKING:
Kristin speaks on career topics such as:
The Four Pillars of Career Fit
Career Management
People Management
Entrepreneurship
Contact mimi@myyoumap.com

PURCHASE YOUMAP® PROFILES:
bit.ly/OrderYouMap

YOUMAP® CERTIFICATIONS:
YouMap® Coach
YouMap® Workshop Facilitator
Visit **www.myyoumap.com** for information

FIND A YOUMAP® COACH OR WORKSHOP FACILTATOR:
www.myyoumap.com/find-a-coach

MEDIA:
Interview Kristin for your radio or TV show, podcast, or print media. She
will deliver fresh insights with practical application for your audience.
Contact mimi@myyoumap.com

Follow on Social Media

LinkedIn: www.linkedin.com/in/kristinsherry

LinkedIn Company Page: http://bit.ly/YouMapLLC

Company Website: www.myyoumap.com

Speaker/Author website: www.kristinsherry.info

Instagram: @myYouMap

Kristin Sherry Twitter: @YouMapCreator

YouMap Twitter: @myYouMap

YouTube Channel: www.youtube.com/c/kristinsherry

OTHER BOOKS BY KRISTIN SHERRY

YouMap: Find Yourself. Blaze Your Path. Show the World!
A step-by-step guide to discover and land a job you'll love.
http://bit.ly/YouMapBook

"YouMap is such a life-changing book that it should be a required reading in all colleges and universities to provide the tools needed at an early age to Finding Yourself, Blazing your Path and Showing the World!! Not only does this book provide the roadmap to discovering YOU and your career best... it also creates clarity, confidence and empowerment to searching for the right job. Thanks to YouMap, I am now on the right career path, but OH how different my life would have been if I had discovered YouMap 25 years ago!! Don't just get one book...buy several for your family and friends! It's one of the best investments you will make for your loved ones." – Amazon review

5 Surprising Steps to Land the Job NOW!
A quick and easy-to-read, value-packed interview prep and performance guide. http://bit.ly/5SurprisingStepstoLandTheJobNOW

"I got the job I wanted! This guide is the perfect combination of comprehensive and concise--74 pages of everything you should think about and prepare for when job hunting. I've never felt so prepared or confident before an interview as I have after reading this book. I wrote down questions detailed in the book verbatim to ask during my interview. I applied to only one position, and I'll be starting my new job soon!" – Amazon review

Follow Your Star: Career Lessons I Learned from Mom
A career empowerment book based on the five success factors for women.
http://bit.ly/FollowYourStarBook

"Encouraging. Educational. Empowering. Kristin Sherry has a wealth of experience in the corporate world and shares her wisdom through storytelling and facts. *Follow Your Star: Career Lessons I Learned from Mom* is a pragmatic yet inspirational read much needed in a world overcrowded with career how-to books. Kristin's authentic and caring personality shines through because she has followed her own star, successfully changed careers and found her true north." – Amazon review

NOTE FROM THE AUTHOR

Word-of-mouth is crucial for any author to succeed. If you enjoyed the book, please leave a review online—anywhere you are able. Even if it's just a sentence or two. It would make all the difference and would be very much appreciated.

Thanks!
Kristin

Thank you so much for reading one of **Kristin A. Sherry's** books.
If you enjoyed the experience, please check out our
recommended title for your next great read!

YouMap by Kristin A. Sherry

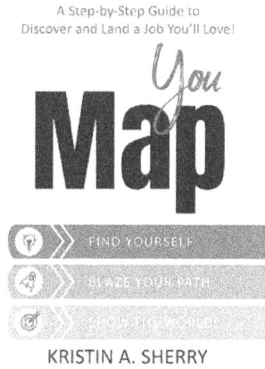

A Step-by-Step Guide to
Discover and Land a Job You'll Love!

You
Map

FIND YOURSELF

BLAZE YOUR PATH

KRISTIN A. SHERRY

"What a fantastic book! Kristin Sherry has done a superb job
narrowing down the steps you need to take to make your
career a more powerful one."
-PAUL CARNEY, entrepreneur, speaker, and author of
Move Your Æ (Ash): Know, Grow, and Show Your Career Value

View other Black Rose Writing titles at
www.blackrosewriting.com/books and use promo code
PRINT to receive a **20% discount** when purchasing.

BLACK ROSE
writing™

www.ingramcontent.com/pod-product-compliance
Lightning Source LLC
Chambersburg PA
CBHW071233210326
41597CB00016B/2040